ST ALBANS CATHEDRAL
WALL PAINTINGS

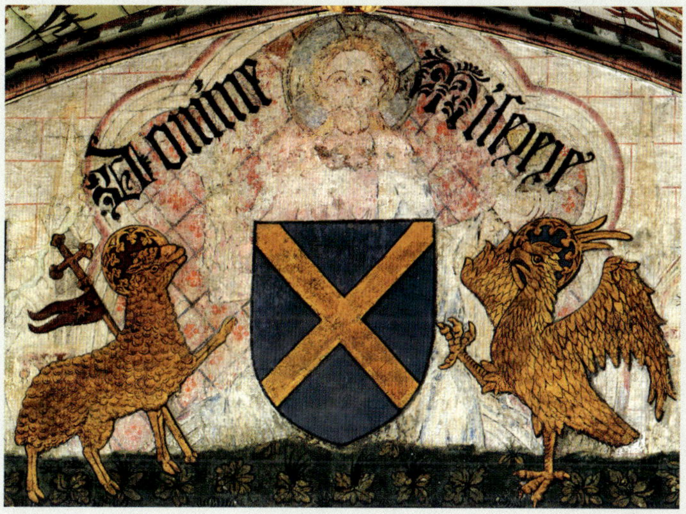

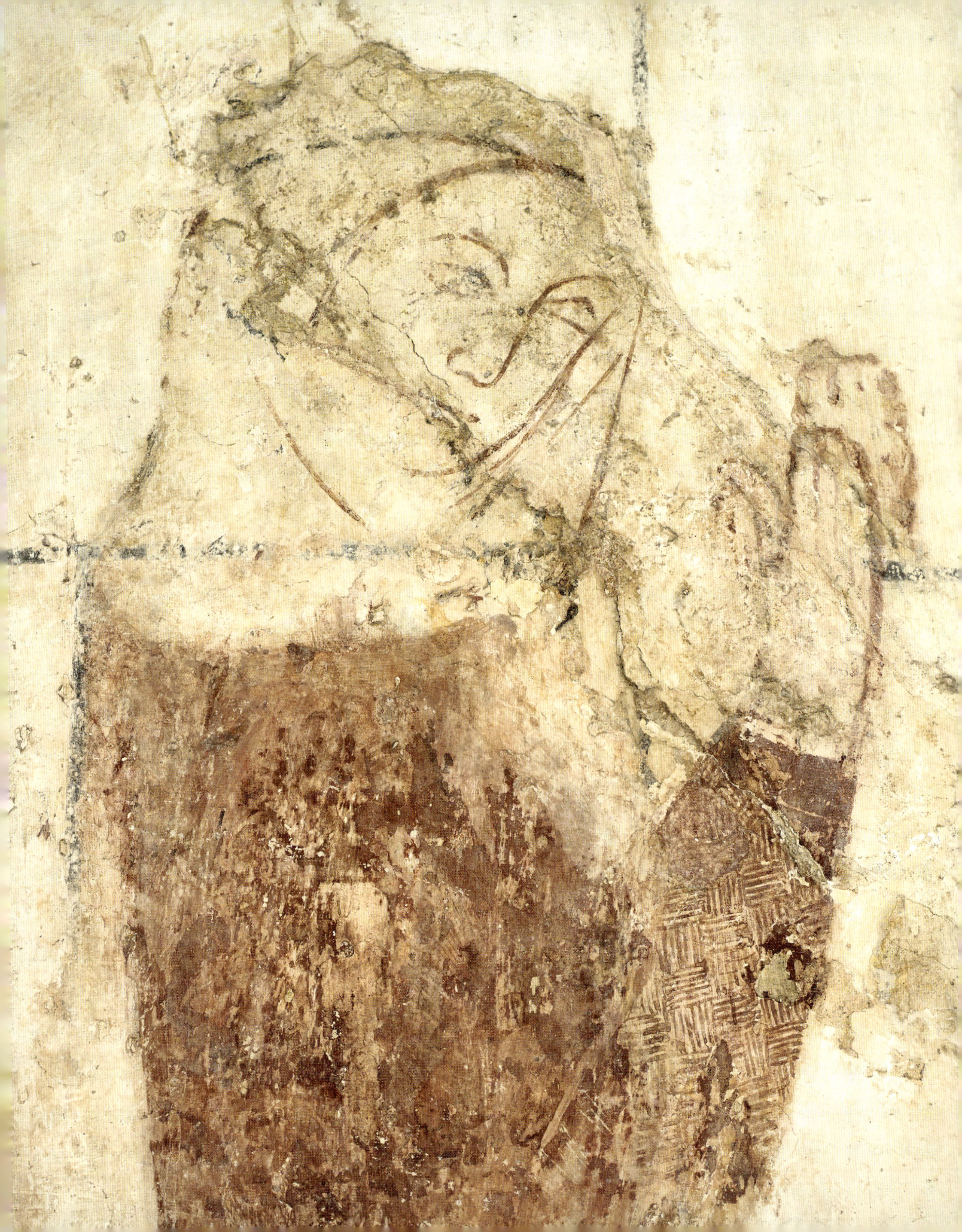

ST ALBANS CATHEDRAL
WALL PAINTINGS

M.A. MICHAEL

ST. ALBANS CATHEDRAL

SCALA

I should like to thank Caroline Barron, Dr Jane Bridgeman, John Goodall, Julia Low, Ailsa Herbert, John McNeill, Nigel Morgan and Craig Williams for their help and advice during the preparation of this text, and Jessica Hodge for her careful editing.

M.A. Michael

Note to the Reader

Dates given for kings are their regnal dates, those for abbots are the dates of their tenure of the abbacy.

First published in 2019 by
Scala Arts and Heritage Publishers Ltd
10 Lion Yard
Tremadoc Road
London SW4 7NQ
www.scalapublishers.com

ISBN 978-1-78551-177-6

Edited by Jessica Hodge
Designed by Raymonde Watkins

Printed and bound in China

10 9 8 7 6 5 4 3 2 1

All photos by Angelo Hornak except:
St Albans Cathedral: pp. 13, 47 (above), 62
The Times / News Licensing: p. 15
© The Victoria and Albert Museum, London: p. 21
British Library, London: pp. 27, 29, 61 (below), 73 (above)
Reproduced by permission of the Master and Fellows of Trinity College Cambridge: p. 37 (both)
Courtesy of the Dean and Chapter, Westminster Abbey: pp. 41, 54
M.A. Michael: p. 43
Courtesy of Stoneyhurst College, Lancs: p. 45
Courtesy of Trinity College, Dublin: p. 47 (below)

CONTENTS

FOREWORD, BY THE VERY REVEREND DR JEFFREY JOHN, DEAN OF ST ALBANS 7

INTRODUCTION **9**

- WALTER OF COLCHESTER AND MATTHEW PARIS 10
- THE WALL PAINTINGS 12
- DISCOVERY, TECHNIQUES AND CONSERVATION 16

THE PAINTINGS **19**

- NAVE 21
- CLERESTORY 50
- TRANSEPTS 52
- CROSSING TOWER 56
- PRESBYTERY 58
- SHRINE CHAPEL OF ST ALBAN 66
- CHANTRY CHAPEL OF HUMPHREY, DUKE OF GLOUCESTER 72

ILLUMINATING THE GREAT NAVE PAINTINGS 74

BIBLIOGRAPHY 78

NOTES 80

GLOSSARY 80

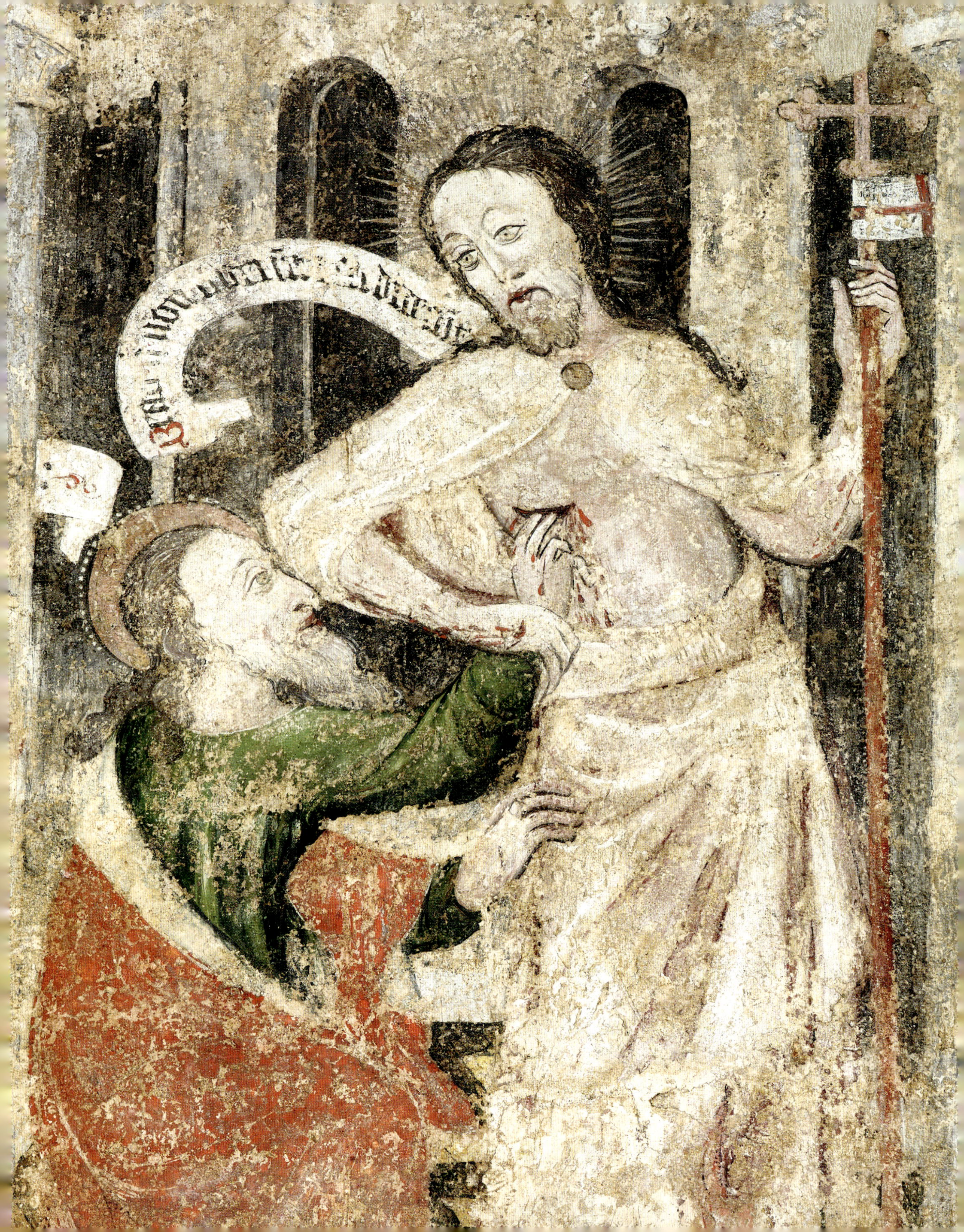

HERE AT ST ALBANS CATHEDRAL WE ARE FORTUNATE to have some of the finest medieval wall paintings in England; no other cathedral has so many, ranging from the Romanesque to the Tudor period. The paintings preserved on the faces of the nave piers represent a unique survival. They inform us about the use of the nave space in the medieval abbey church in important ways that relate to practices more often found in parish churches.

Through the previous research work of Dr Eileen Roberts, we began to understand the importance of our collection. In this new publication, Dr Michael delves more deeply into their history and significance and, aided by the wonderful photographs by Angelo Hornak, we are now able to share more of the story of the paintings with a wider audience.

We have long wanted to lift the veil of time to see how the paintings might have appeared when they were freshly executed. Through the generosity of the National Lottery Heritage Fund, we have now been able to recreate the four large images in the nave by using light projection, the first project of this kind inside a medieval cathedral in England. They help us understand why pilgrims of the Middle Ages, on entering the abbey at the end of their journey, are said to have fallen to their knees in wonder, believing they had entered heaven itself.

The Very Reverend Jeffrey John
Dean of St Albans

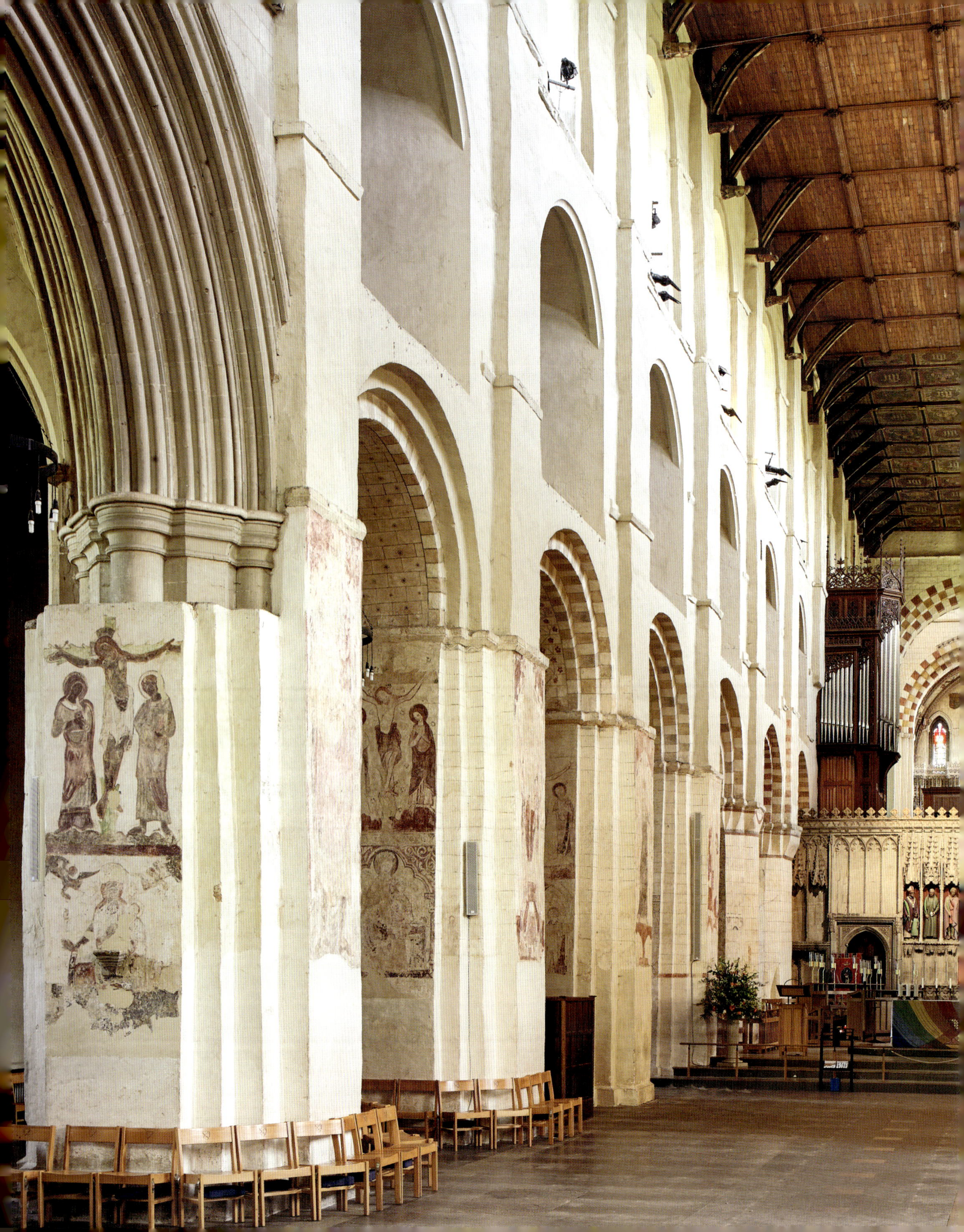

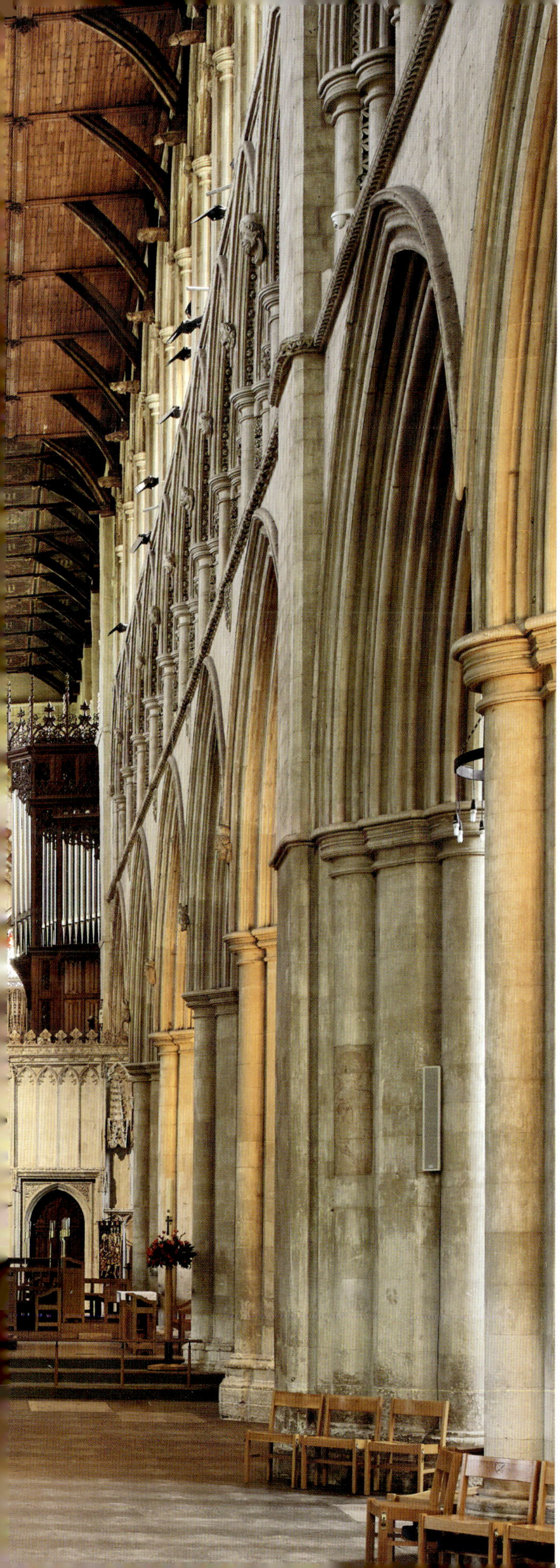

INTRODUCTION

According to the tradition recorded by the St Albans monk, historian, diplomat and artist Matthew Paris (1200–59) in his *Lives of the Offas*, the abbey was founded around 793 by the Mercian king Offa in honour of Alban, a Roman citizen, who was regarded as the first Christian to be martyred in Britain.[1] The earliest written references to Alban's life were made by the British authors Gildas (500–570) and Bede (672–735), who appear to have based their work on a late antique *Passio* (*Passion*) of St Alban, which was probably written *c.* 429 when St Germanus travelled to Britain from France and collected relics of the saint.[2] This suggests that Alban was probably martyred in the early fourth century but the exact date is unknown. A basilica was dedicated to Alban by St Germanus in Auxerre and a series of text panels appear to have been displayed there, perhaps with pictures that may have been the earliest images of the saint.[3]

Some fragments of plaster have survived from the Anglo-Saxon abbey, suggesting that it had at least a simple scheme of decorative painting before it was rebuilt under Abbot Paul of Caen (1077–93), after the Norman conquest.[4] From this time onwards St Albans Abbey gained a privileged status among the religious houses in England. Its position on the main road out of London made it an important resting place for kings and prelates on their journeys north. It gained particular favour during the reign of Henry III (1216–72) and his son Edward I (1272–1307), a status it did not lose until the dissolution of the monasteries in the sixteenth century. Henry III often stayed for several nights, bestowing gifts of silks and jewels on the shrine of St Alban.[5] It was during his reign that Matthew Paris wrote and illuminated his major works here and some of the most important wall paintings that have survived at St Albans were executed.

The nave looking east to the fourteenth-century nave screen and presbytery beyond. The first painted pier (fourth from the west end of the nave) retains its original eleventh-century lower half, the earliest figurative painting to have survived at St Albans.

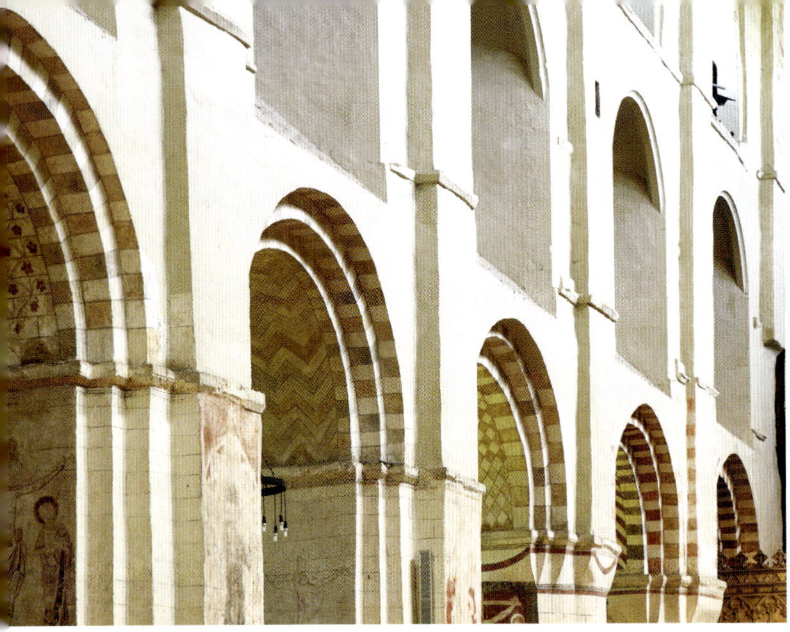

The north arcade of the nave, built between 1077 and 1089, retains its original painting of red, yellow-grey and white imitation masonry blocks.

(opposite)
The stepped profiles of the arches of the north arcade of the nave display patterns of chevrons and alternating grey (originally black) and red blocks imitating stone.

WALTER OF COLCHESTER AND MATTHEW PARIS

The earliest paintings are recorded during the abbacies of John of Cella (1195–1214) and William of Trumpington (1214–35), when Master Walter of Colchester (died 1248), a monk of St Albans – together with his brother Simon, who was not a monk, and his nephew Richard – is credited in the *Gesta Abbatum* (*Deeds of the Abbots*) of St Albans with having painted '*tabulae*' (probably altar frontals) for the church.[6] We are told that Brother Ralph Gubiun of Dunstable (*c.* 1180–1200), who produced a Latin verse *Life of St Alban*, persuaded Walter to become a monk,[7] suggesting that he had already trained as an artist before he joined the community.[8] He appears to have been an exceptionally gifted goldsmith, sculptor and painter and is credited with decorating a 'beam on which the history of St Alban figured' above the high altar.[9] Matthew Paris calls him *'sculptor et pictor incomparabilis'*, the term *pictor* here having the sense of image-maker as much as painter. Walter was later called upon to provide metalwork images for the shrine of St Thomas at Canterbury, for which Henry III allowed funds to be allocated from the archbishopric.[10] As William Lethaby suggested in 1916, it is tempting to associate at least one of the wall paintings at St Albans – the first painted pier – with Walter's name.[11] This idea is supported by Abbot John of Cella's decision not to destroy the lower part of the pier when he instigated the western extension of the nave in the new gothic style, work that was finished *c.* 1224.[12] The respect that Matthew Paris gives Walter – he also calls him *pictor praeelectus* (preeminent painter) – may explain why the lower part of the pier was not remodelled.

Matthew Paris was admitted as a monk in 1217, two years after Walter was made sacrist. If the eulogy by Thomas of Walsingham (1370–1422) to Matthew (added to the *Gesta Abbatum* nearly a century and a half after his death in 1259) is to be believed, he may also have been trained as an artist, if not as a goldsmith, by Walter of Colchester.[13] Matthew is now remembered for his illustrated Latin chronicles of England and lives of saints, including his translations into Anglo-Norman French of the lives of St Alban[14] and St Edmund of Abingdon (died 1240, canonised 1246). The latter was made for presentation to Isabel, Countess of Arundel (1228–82), with whom Matthew was in correspondence concerning the loan of manuscript lives of St Thomas of Canterbury and St Edward the Confessor, which he was evidently supplying.[15] The idea that there was a 'school of mural painting and manuscript illumination' at St Albans is, however, no longer accepted, and Matthew is now regarded as gifted amateur,[16] whereas Walter of Colchester and his family should certainly be regarded as professional artists. Comparisons between the psalter given to the abbey by the St Albans monk John of Dalling (see p. 27) and the images on the second painted pier suggest that manuscripts

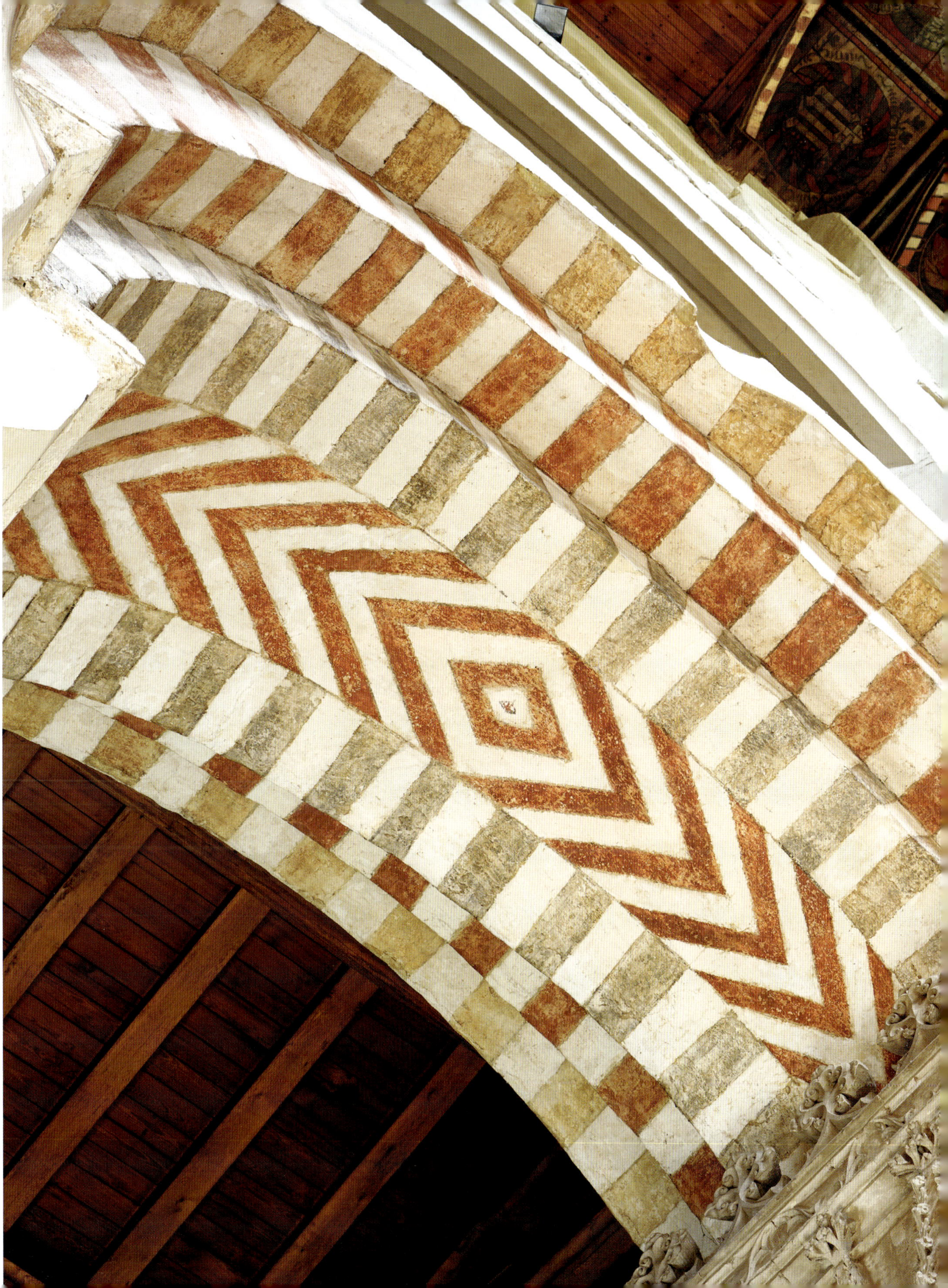

produced for the community were made by artists who themselves knew the wall paintings and drew on them for inspiration.[17] From the quality of the work that has survived at St Albans, it appears that Walter's reputation and Matthew's contacts in court circles led to some of the most sought-after artists of the thirteenth and early fourteenth centuries being called upon to execute murals at St Albans.

THE WALL PAINTINGS

A striking feature of the architecture of St Albans abbey is the contrast between the monumental Romanesque round-headed arches of the north side of the nave and crossing and the pointed gothic arches of the south side of the nave, presbytery and Lady Chapel. The organic way in which the architectural style developed at St Albans over time, however, has left a legacy of wall painting that provides a unique picture of how the decoration of an abbey church would have functioned in the Middle Ages. The quantity of wall paintings that have survived, from decorative painting to figurative work, inscriptions and heraldry, and ranging in date from the thirteenth to the sixteenth century, is exceptional in England. It is rivalled only by the survivals at the great churches of Winchester, Norwich, Durham and Westminster. There is a long tradition in the Church, stemming from comments made by Pope Gregory the Great (590–604), that wall paintings – particularly when displaying the iconography of the liturgical year or the lives of saints – acted as bibles for the poor, but this is often not borne out by the

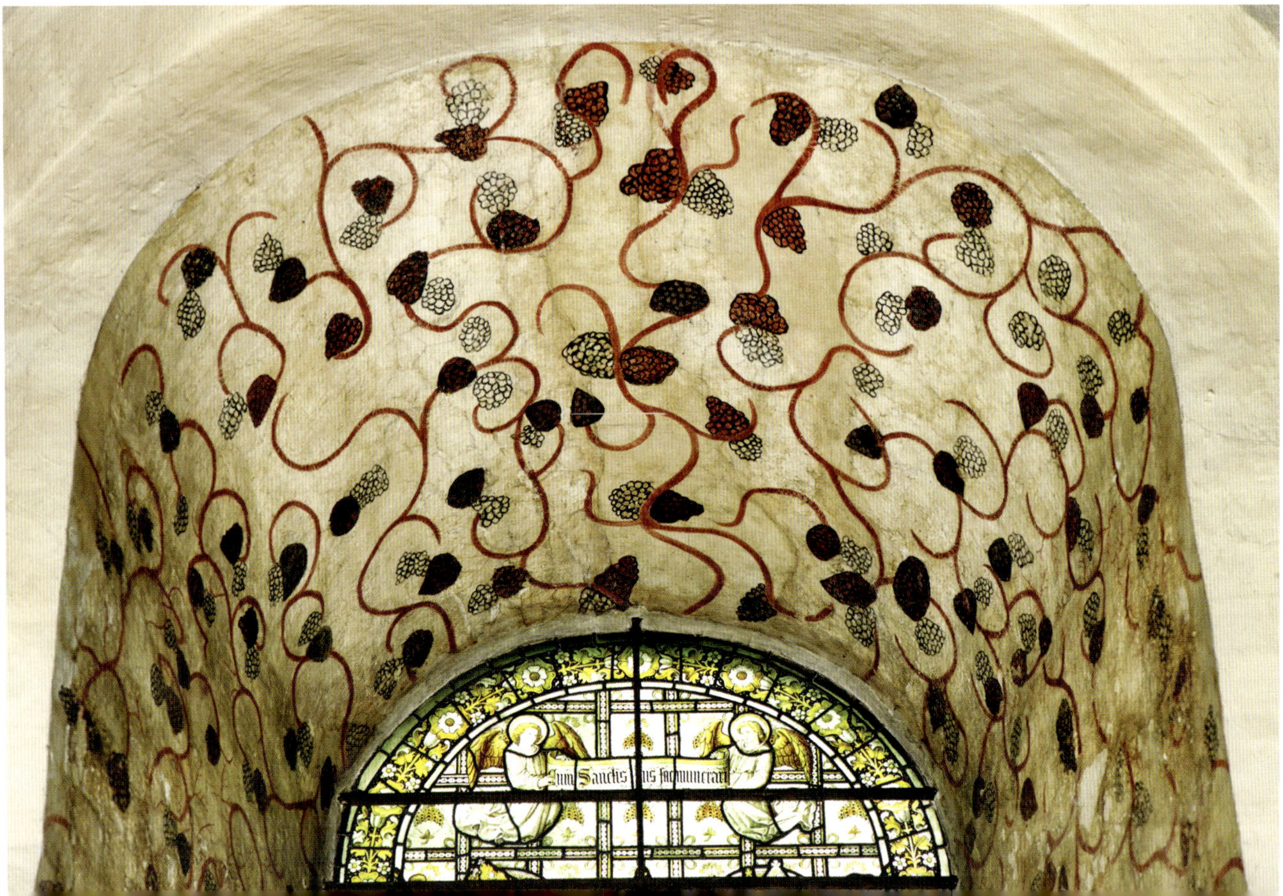

The splay of this Romanesque window in the north transept, above a small door used by pilgrims entering the church via the town Waxhouse Gate, was painted in the fifteenth or early sixteenth century with a design of white and red grapes. The vine is a common eucharistic symbol.

evidence of the paintings themselves.[18] Pre-Reformation wall paintings serve rather as an expression of a deeply Christian culture in which the spaces in the church acted as sites for prayer and devotion, in the expectation of redemption from sin, and could reflect the particular dedications of individuals. They could also hold an apotropaic (harm-averting) meaning, denoting the holiness of particular spaces and protection from evil. This desire to be associated with a holy place could also be said to apply to Protestant memorials, such as the rare painted image of Ralph Maynard (died 1613) on the south aisle wall of the presbytery, praying to a light that bursts through cloud and bears the name of God written in Hebrew (*Yahweh*) and Latin (*Deus*).[19]

The Romanesque decorative schemes can still be seen in many parts of the church; the use of chevrons on the underside of the Romanesque arches, the rosettes and the alternating red or yellow and white of the imitation blocks of stone can be paralleled in many of the surviving great churches in England, but walls that are plastered over rough infill or poorly coursed stone are painted with lines, to create the impression of stone blocks. At St Albans the surviving paintings on the upper walls of the crossing tower and its arches, and the decoration of the six Romanesque bays on the north side of the nave as well as in the presbytery, suggest that the whole abbey was originally unified through this type of painted decoration.

Of the twelve piers on the north side of the abbey, nine survive from the Romanesque church. All were painted between the last years of the twelfth century and the fourteenth. The nave screen, which was erected in the middle of the fourteenth century, prevents a view of the ninth and tenth piers from the west, but recently uncovered paintings on the eleventh and twelfth piers indicate that between 1190 and 1350 all the surviving Romanesque piers were painted. When two of the piers on the south side collapsed in 1323, they dragged down five bays with them, and had to be reconstructed. The elaborate and multifaceted surfaces of the new gothic architecture changed the way painting could be displayed on these piers. The system of flat or gently curved surfaces used on the earlier piers could not now be replicated on the south side of the nave, but the painting on the fifth nave pier, although rebuilt, still retained its flat pilaster strip, on which the traces of a fourteenth-century image of the Virgin and Child survives across its remodelled shafts (p. 49). This is because the chapel of the Blessed Virgin at the Pillar, set up by the monk William Wyntyrshulle in the early fifteenth century, appears to have stood between the fifth and sixth piers on the south side of the nave.[20]

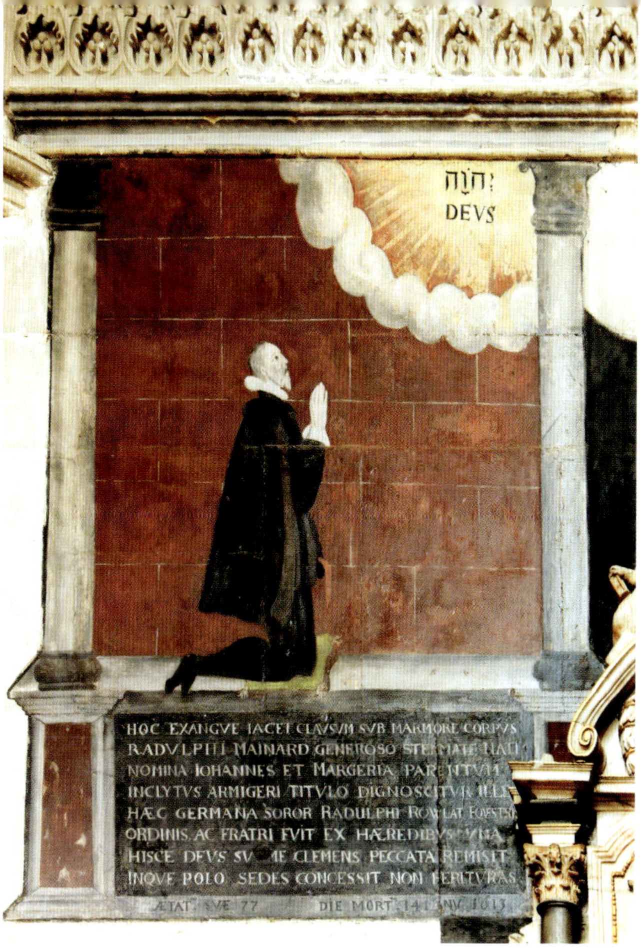

Memorial to Ralph Maynard (died 1613), placed high up on the wall of the presbytery south aisle. He is depicted in a black cloak and white ruff, kneeling between two columns and praying to the name of God written in Hebrew and Latin, rather than to an image of God, as he belonged to a prominent Protestant family.

The iconography of the scenes that survive on the north side of the nave tells a story of votive devotion rather than instruction. Each pier appears to have been paid for by a separate donor. The first five depict the Crucifixion, above the Virgin and Child, the Annunciation or the Coronation of the Virgin; the sixth may have displayed a Trinity image, which has disappeared. By the thirteenth century it was necessary for most monks to say mass daily and so the number of altars grew, but these wall paintings did not serve as altarpieces in themselves; they were not designed to function liturgically, although altars would have been placed below them.[21] Like the many private devotional paintings and ivories that have survived from the thirteenth and fourteenth centuries, they functioned rather as intercessionary images (see p. 21). Donors – probably initially monks, but later also members of the laity – would have given money to the abbey for the images to be painted. The scroll bearing a prayer carried by one of the donors is still visible on the first painted pier (p. 23) and may have been painted when Walter of Colchester and his family were working at the abbey. Stylistically this is related to illuminated manuscripts produced *c.* 1200–30, such as the English Psalter in Munich.[22]

High in the wall space between the clerestory windows, immediately beyond the fourteenth-century nave screen, a series of what appears to be standing apostles and, perhaps, prophets still survives (p. 50). Such displays of apostles, prophets or ancestors of Christ formed part of the iconography of the upper reaches of great churches in stained glass as well as in wall painting. They have an apotropaic or protective function as guardians of the upper reaches of the quire. Their purpose was not instructive, although three can be identified from their attributes as St James and, possibly, St John the Evangelist and St Thomas Apostle. The paintings on the south faces of the north nave piers tell a similar story of individual patronage and devotion. The laity who attended the lost parochial chapel of St Andrew on the north side of the nave were being buried in the nave by the fourteenth century. Surviving fragmentary inscriptions on the lower parts of the piers provide evidence of their donations of money for the upkeep of these paintings.[23] Inscriptions and donor figures can be made out below or near the grand (but damaged)

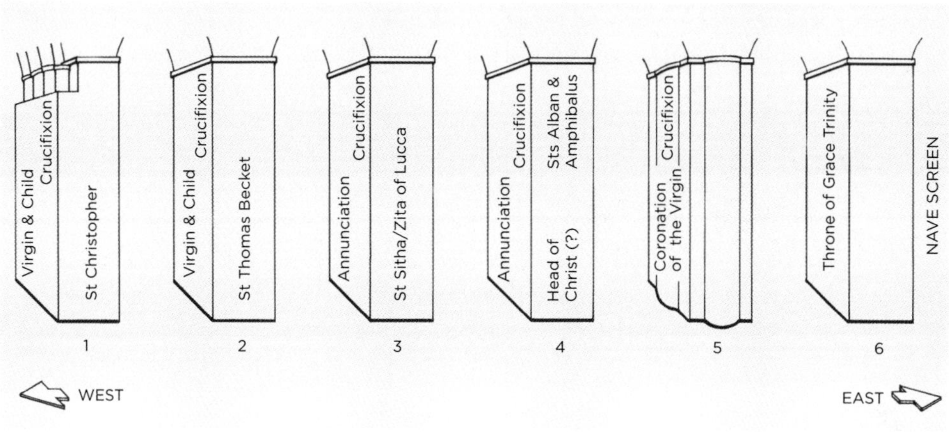

Diagram to show the position of the paintings on the painted piers in the north nave arcade.

figures of St Christopher, St Thomas Becket and St Sitha (pp. 40–45), which would once have greeted those entering the parochial chapel or attending mass in the nave. The narrative image of Sts Alban and Amphibalus on the fourth painted pier (p. 46) was probably placed there in the late thirteenth century because the shrine of St Amphibalus was once housed behind a protective iron railing near the altar of the Holy Cross, close to the nave screen before this was moved (after the collapse of the southern piers of the nave in 1323) to a position in the vestibule to the east of the chapel that housed the shrine of St Alban.[24]

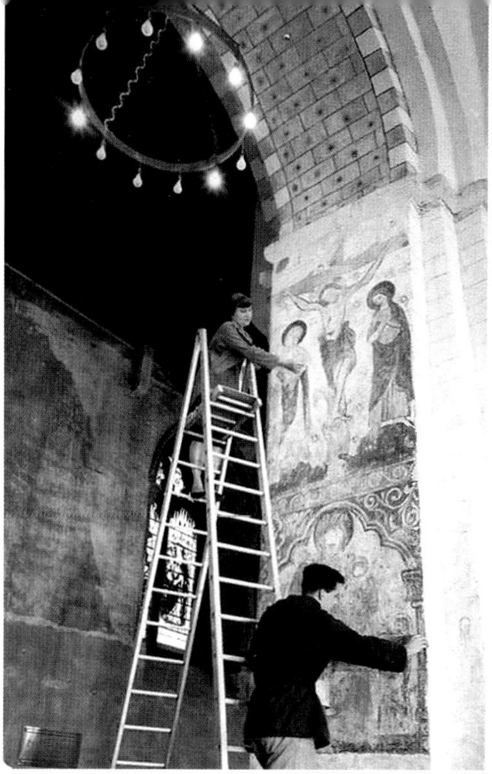

The conservators Eve and Robert Baker working on the painted piers in the nave, August 1960.

A description of the site of the altars, monuments and tombs, as well as of the 'Pictures and Images placed near the Altar of the Holy Cross in the Church of the Monastery of St Alban' was written in 1428 by John Amundesham, about whom little else is known. He may have been a high-ranking lay brother or amanuensis of Abbot Wheathampstead during his first abbacy (1420–40).[25] He describes an altar 'placed near the public path where many persons pass and go out' which displays two columns, one an earth colour and the other red, topped by a 'tower of charity' and a 'tower of honour'; these had the instruments of the Passion emblazoned on them and the Passion and Resurrection were depicted above the altar. The Latin text refers to these images as the 'History of the Passion' (below) and the 'History of the Resurrection' (above). It is now assumed that the surviving Doubting of St Thomas (p. 53) should be identified with the 'History of the Resurrection'; the lower painting was destroyed when the pilaster strip was removed. Amundesham appears to describe a highly complicated and diagrammatic set of images, similar to surviving images from contemporary illuminated manuscripts, which were almost certainly derived from didactic works such as Master John of Metz's *Mirror of Theology* (1273).[26] It is significant that Amundesham's text includes references to Pope Gregory the Great's defence of images – 'they who are unlearned may read by only looking on the walls'.[27] Nevertheless, he is careful to include the proviso 'and if anyone wishes to make images, forbid him not, but by all means avoid worshipping'. This statement must be directed at the laity, who would not just pass through the north transept as pilgrims, but also pray at the second altar of the Holy Cross (also known as the Leaning Cross) in the north transept and at the nearby altar of St Sitha.[28] Amundesham's Latin text was certainly designed for the monks rather than the laity to read, but it is also a rebuff to the iconoclastic teachings of John Wycliffe (died 1384) and his Lollardy movement. Thomas of Walsingham's chronicle records that 'poisonous Lollard tracts' were distributed in St Albans in 1417 and Abbot John of Wheathampstead (1452–65) issued ordinances against '*pseudo-predicatores*' (fake preachers).[29] In this context the text may have been designed as a form of guide to help the monks explain the meaning of the imagery to pilgrims. Such descriptive texts have also survived for Canterbury Cathedral, to explain the complicated iconography of its stained-glass windows.[30]

DISCOVERY, TECHNIQUES AND CONSERVATION

Most of the paintings at St Albans, having been whitewashed during the Reformation, were uncovered after 1862 but the Doubting of St Thomas appears to have been found earlier, in 1846, and the bishop on the north-east wall of the shrine chapel of St Alban was discovered by the rector, Dr Henry J .B. Nicholson, in 1848.[31] The Crucifixion in the chantry chapel of Humphrey, Duke of Gloucester (1390–1447) had been known to antiquarians since 1703 and was later engraved in Richard Gough's *Sepulchral Monuments* in 1796.[32]

The figure of the bishop painted in the shrine chapel of St Alban (p. 66) is accompanied by an archbishop, uncovered more recently on the south side. Both were part of long retables (decorative altar backs) that once graced altars on either side of the entrance to the chapel.[33] The artists who painted these images were familiar with the latest trends in painting at the royal court in London between 1270 and 1320 and may also have been employed to apply painted decoration to the shrine of St Alban. Their technique of multiple layers of paint, utilising linseed oil as a medium, gives these paintings a luminosity that is only matched at St Albans by the Doubting of St Thomas in the north transept. Nearly all the other paintings that have survived here were painted on a thin layer of limewash, using the simple earth colours of red and yellow ochres as well as white lead, vermillion and malachite. This was done not in the wet plaster *fresco* technique of Italy, but in *secco*, dry surface painting, which in northern Europe even at this early date might also include layers of oil paint. Only the painting on the first painted pier, associated with Master Walter of Colchester, has a thicker limewash that has bonded to the plaster in a manner comparable to *fresco* technique.[34]

It is difficult to know how much colour was applied to the final layers of the paintings, partly because the first attempts to conserve them proved misguided. Many were revealed by crude scraping during the rectorship of Dr Nicholson and were treated with varnish. By 1902 this had to be stabilised and William Page 'applied a specially prepared size, warm, to the flakes of varnish ... by dabbing them ...', remarking that 'it was rather a trial of patience'.[35] Later still, in the 1930s, Professor Ernest W. Tristram, whose publications enlarged upon the work of Charles Keyser in the 1880s, conserved a great many of the paintings.[36] He applied a layer of wax in order to fix and preserve the colour which, although successful in some cases, did not allow the paintings to breathe and also discoloured. In 1955 Eve and Robert Baker and their conservation team began remedial work to remove the wax, and further work has been carried out since 1992 by the Perry Lithgow Partnership and the Courtauld Institute Conservation of Wall Paintings Department.[37] The care of the paintings is now an ongoing concern in order to preserve them for future generations.

The archbishop figure on the south side of the shrine of St Alban (detail).

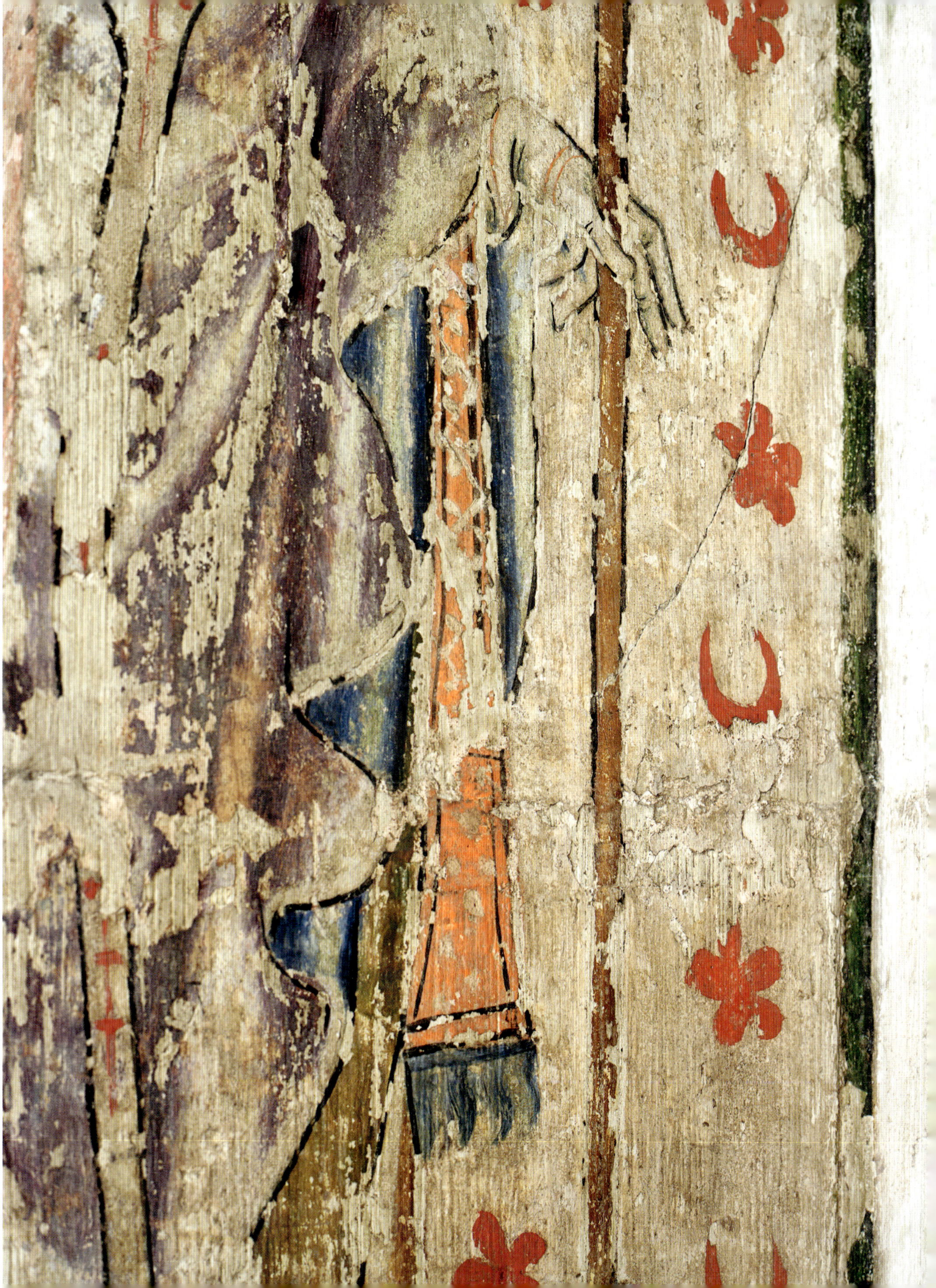

THE PAINTINGS

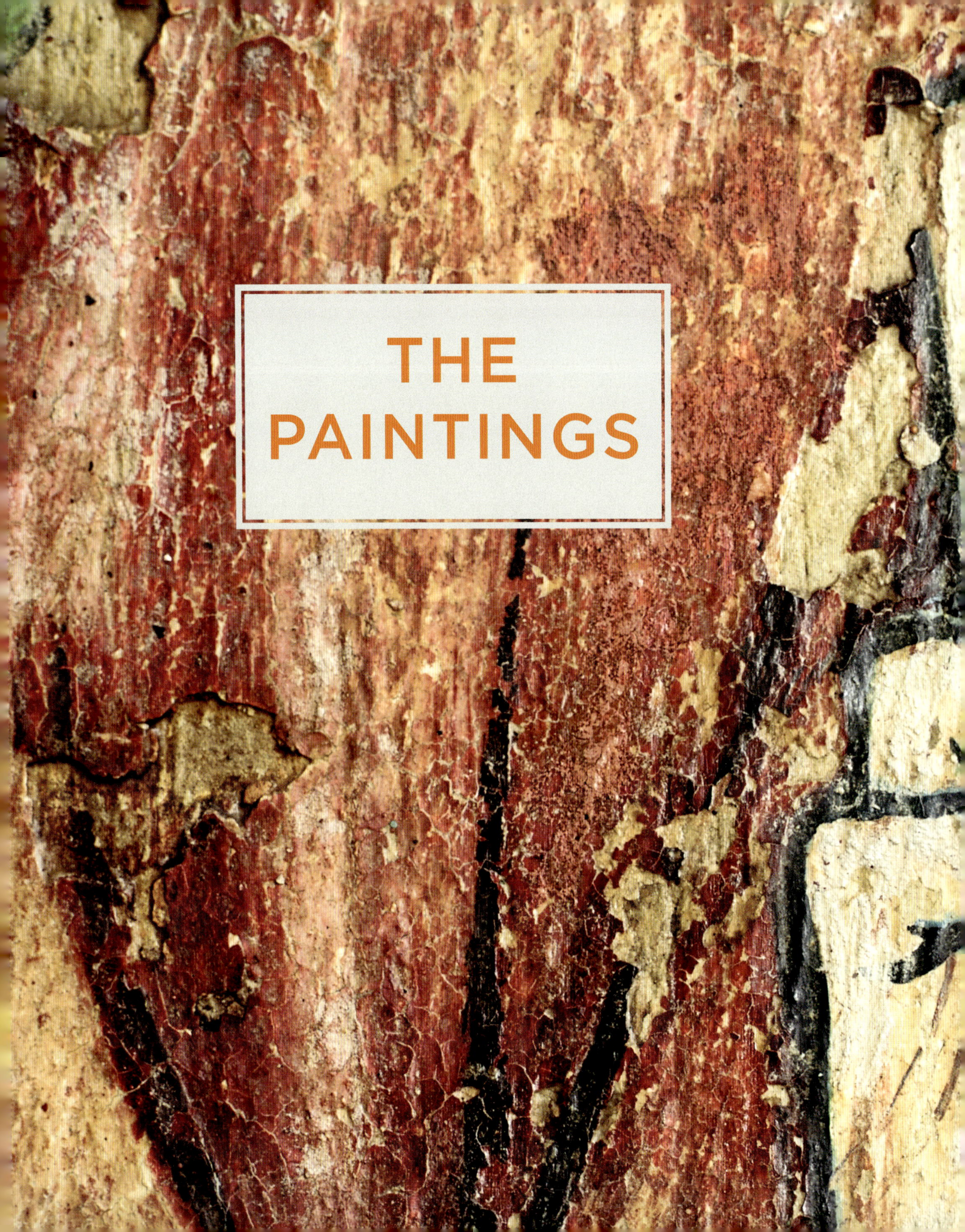

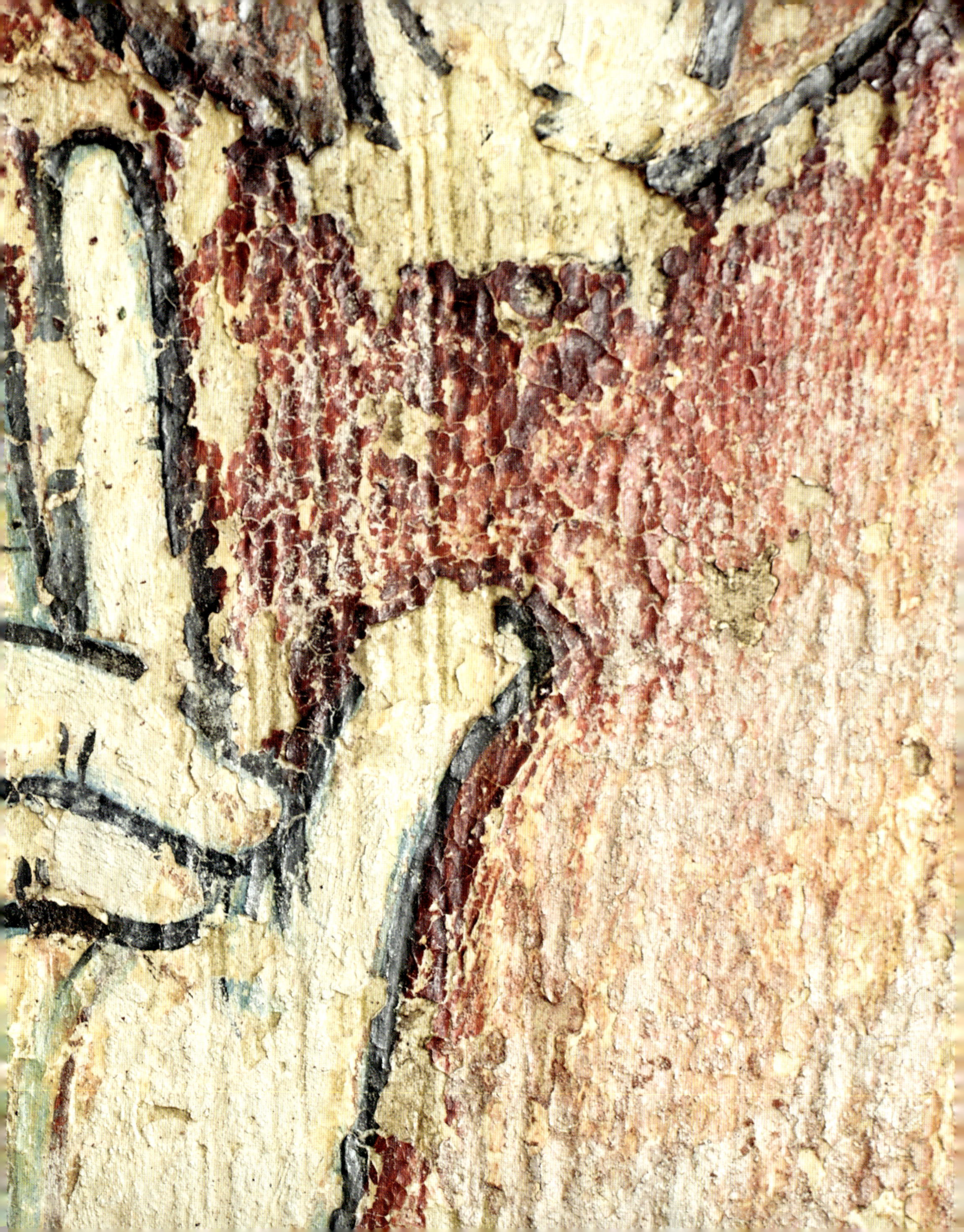

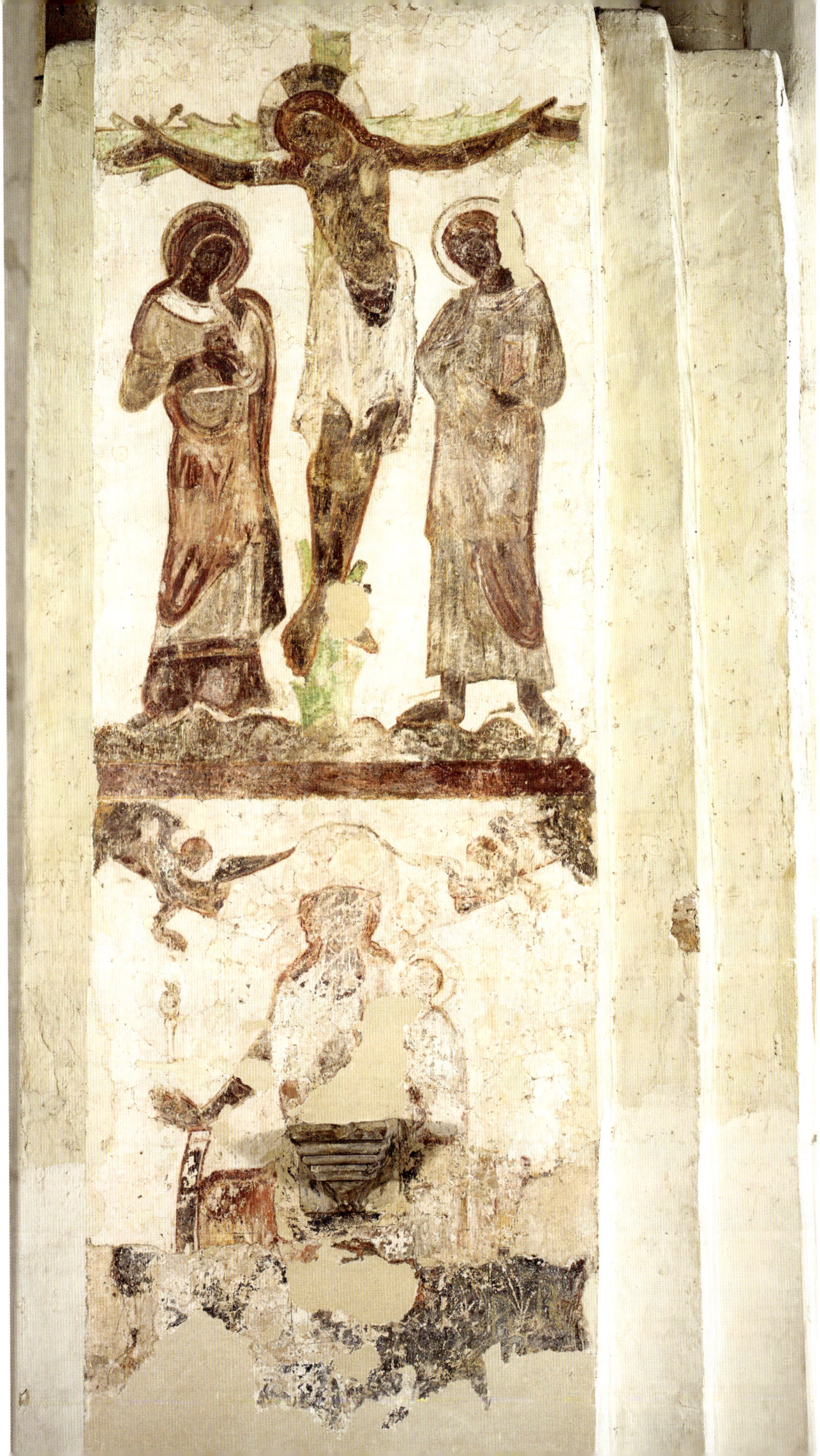

CRUCIFIXION AND VIRGIN AND CHILD

Only the lower part of this pier displaying the Crucifixion and the Virgin and Child belongs to the building of Abbot Paul of Caen. The thirteenth-century masonry pattern that is seen below all the other images on painted piers in the nave is absent, and a different thickness of limewash is used. This suggests that it is the earliest of the images, possibly dating to *c.* 1190–1220 and painted either before or during the building works. That it has survived, and acted as an iconographical model for the following two piers, suggests that it may have been identified as the work of Walter of Colchester, whose name occurs frequently in the chronicles of St Albans at this time. We know that Walter was a professional artist who was persuaded to join the community by Brother Ralph Gubiun, and that he brought his brother Simon and nephew Richard to St Albans to help with the painting of the abbey. Matthew Paris tells us that Abbot William of Trumpington wanted to make continual use of him 'while he was alive and flourishing ... for we do not remember seeing his equal in all kinds of skills nor do we believe that anyone will equal him in the future.'[38]

Below the Virgin and Child, part of the figure of the donor can still be seen kneeling on the left-hand side of the throne. A scroll, which would have contained a prayer asking the Virgin to intercede for him so that his prayer could reach Christ, rises up to meet her hand, which carries a flowering rod symbolic of her purity and authority as Queen of Heaven. The donor may well have been Abbot Trumpington, or another member of the community.

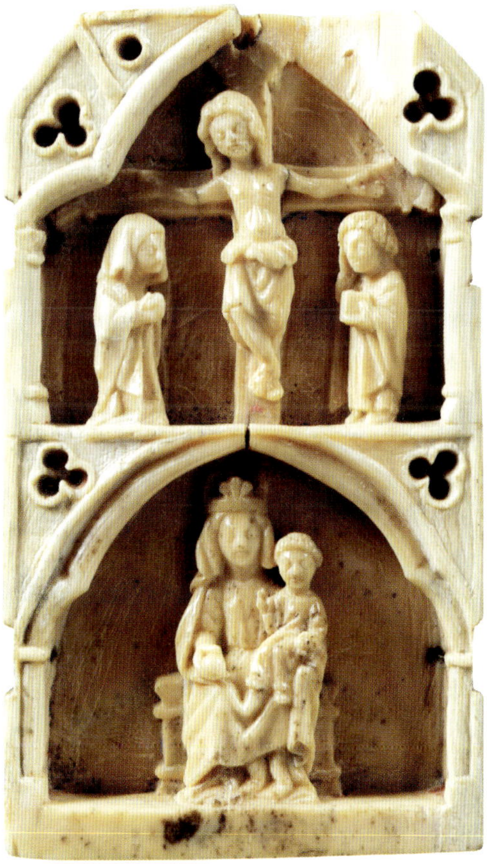

CRUCIFIXION AND VIRGIN AND CHILD

This small ivory, carved from a walrus tusk, was found in 1853 on the site of the abbey of St Clare in Haydon Square, London (now destroyed), and is a rare surviving example of English ivory carving from the third quarter of the thirteenth century. A portable object measuring only 7.8 × 4.5 cm, it once had wings to enable it to be closed. It is further evidence for the juxtaposition of Christ's sacrifice with the Virgin, through whom prayers of intercession could be made to Christ; the same arrangement of Crucifixion and Virgin and Child as on the first and second painted piers. This iconography, often as a diptych (with images side by side), is also found in private devotional works in panel painting, as well as in small enamel and metalwork objects that could be worn by the owner.

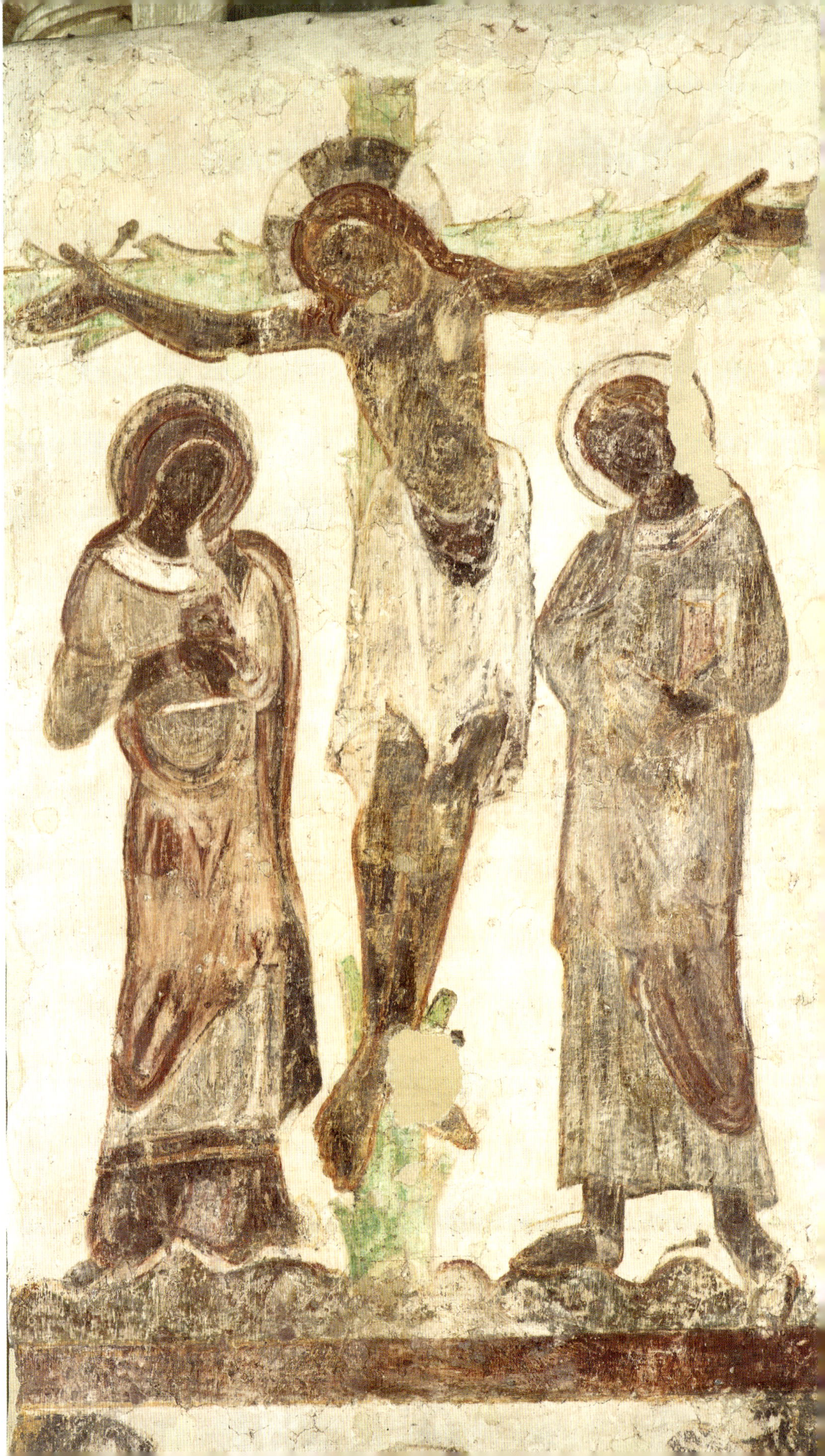

CRUCIFIXION

The flesh tones have darkened owing to discoloration of red lead pigment. The malachite green of the of the so-called 'raguly' or 'lopped branch' cross symbolises rebirth, an iconography known since Anglo-Saxon times and referred to in the Middle English poem *'Cursor Mundi'*.

VIRGIN AND CHILD

Despite being deliberately preserved after the remodelling of the nave in the early thirteenth century, this painting was evidently whitewashed *c.* 1400, when the plinth was inserted at its centre to hold a statue of St Richard of Chichester. Censing angels descend from clouds at the top left and right and the scroll once carrying a prayer from a kneeling donor can be seen on the left, below the Virgin's hand. The frontality of the Virgin's pose recalls surviving thirteenth-century painted wooden sculpture and ivory carving from Scandinavia and Germany, as well as English illuminated manuscripts.[39] The flowering rod she carries has regal connotations and also refers to the prophecy of Isaiah in the Old Testament (11:1): 'And there shall come forth a rod out of the stem of Jesse, and a branch shall grow out of his roots.'

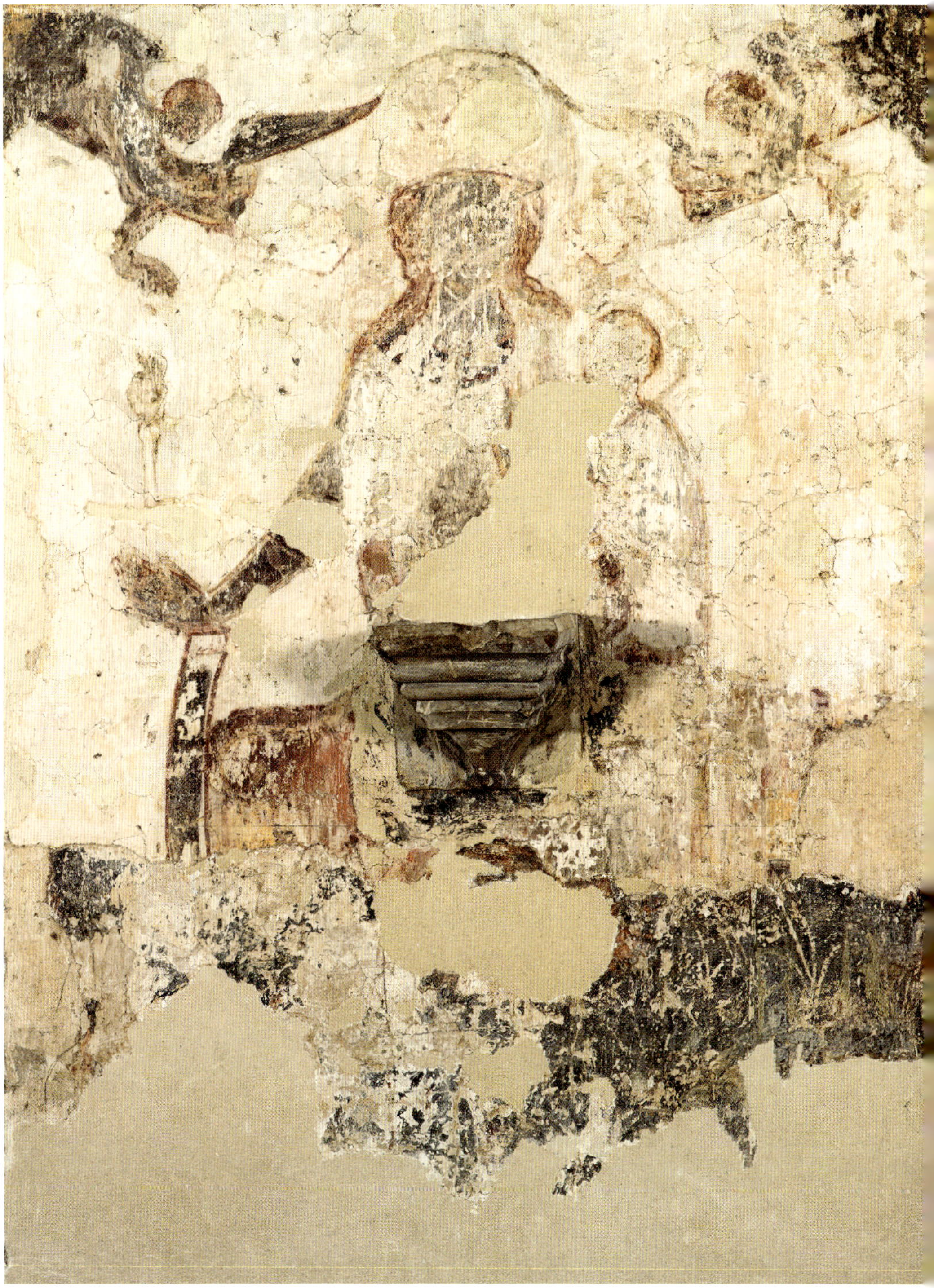

CRUCIFIXION AND VIRGIN AND CHILD

The second painted pier presents a very different view of the Crucifixion. Christ is shown with crossed legs to facilitate the use of a single nail, rather than the two used on the first painted pier; this convention, which suggests a Trinitarian interpretation of the nails, became the norm in the later thirteenth century. The iconography of the living 'lopped branch' cross is again used, but the body of Christ now hangs lower than the branches of the cross. On the right-hand side of the Virgin's throne below, the image of a haloed figure may be discerned. Professor Ernest Tristram, who conserved the paintings at St Albans in the 1930s, believed this to be an addition and suggested that it represented St Benedict, as the halo means it cannot be a donor. A more likely interpretation is that it is part of the original painting and represents a censing angel, an image found frequently both in the wall paintings at St Albans and in illuminated manuscripts. The Virgin and Child and the Crucifixion both bear a striking resemblance to images of the same subjects found in the monk John of Dalling's psalter, made *c.* 1250 (see p. 27). The lines of the thirteenth-century masonry pattern are visible below and to either side of the image, as can the fourteenth-century head of a female figure at the bottom right of the pier. This suggests that this pier did not receive its images until after the masonry pattern was completed, probably 40 or 50 years after the painting of the first pier, which has no such pattern and belongs to a previous campaign of decoration.

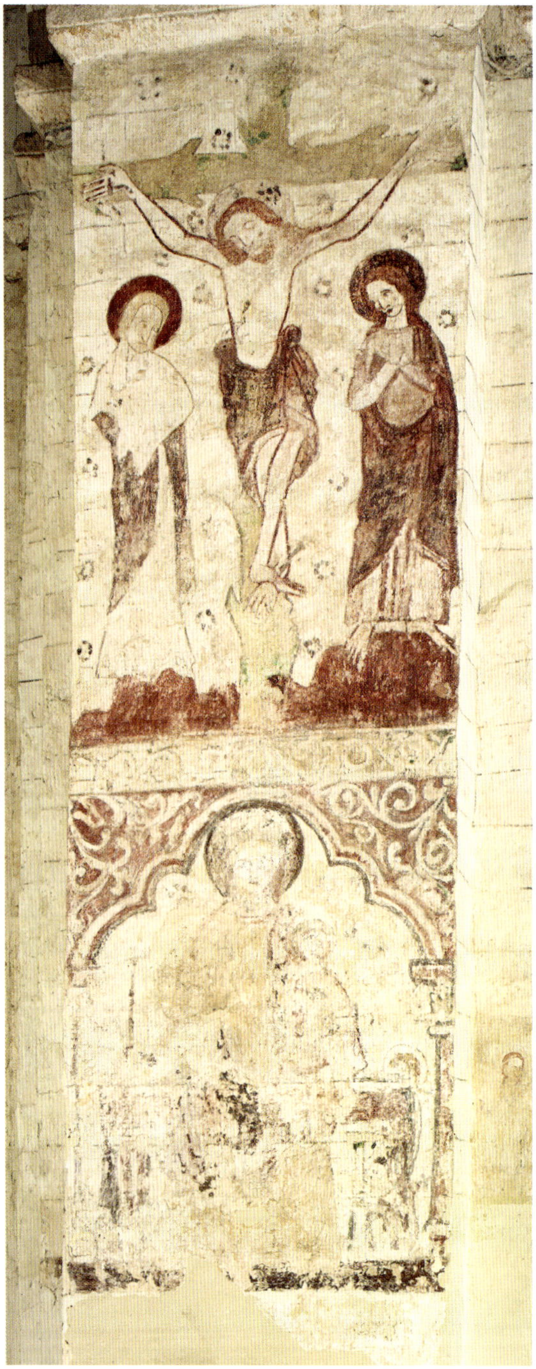

CRUCIFIXION

The growing interest in the humanity of Christ during the thirteenth century is seen here in the depiction of his body as thin and vulnerable. His suffering is accentuated by the crossed legs and the attenuated arms, which carry a realistically heavy weight supported by the nails. Although the faces appear to have been partly redrawn, perhaps during Tristram's restoration in the 1930s, the composition makes a striking contrast to the formality of the image on the first painted pier, where Christ's body is displayed frontally and with only a slight curve.

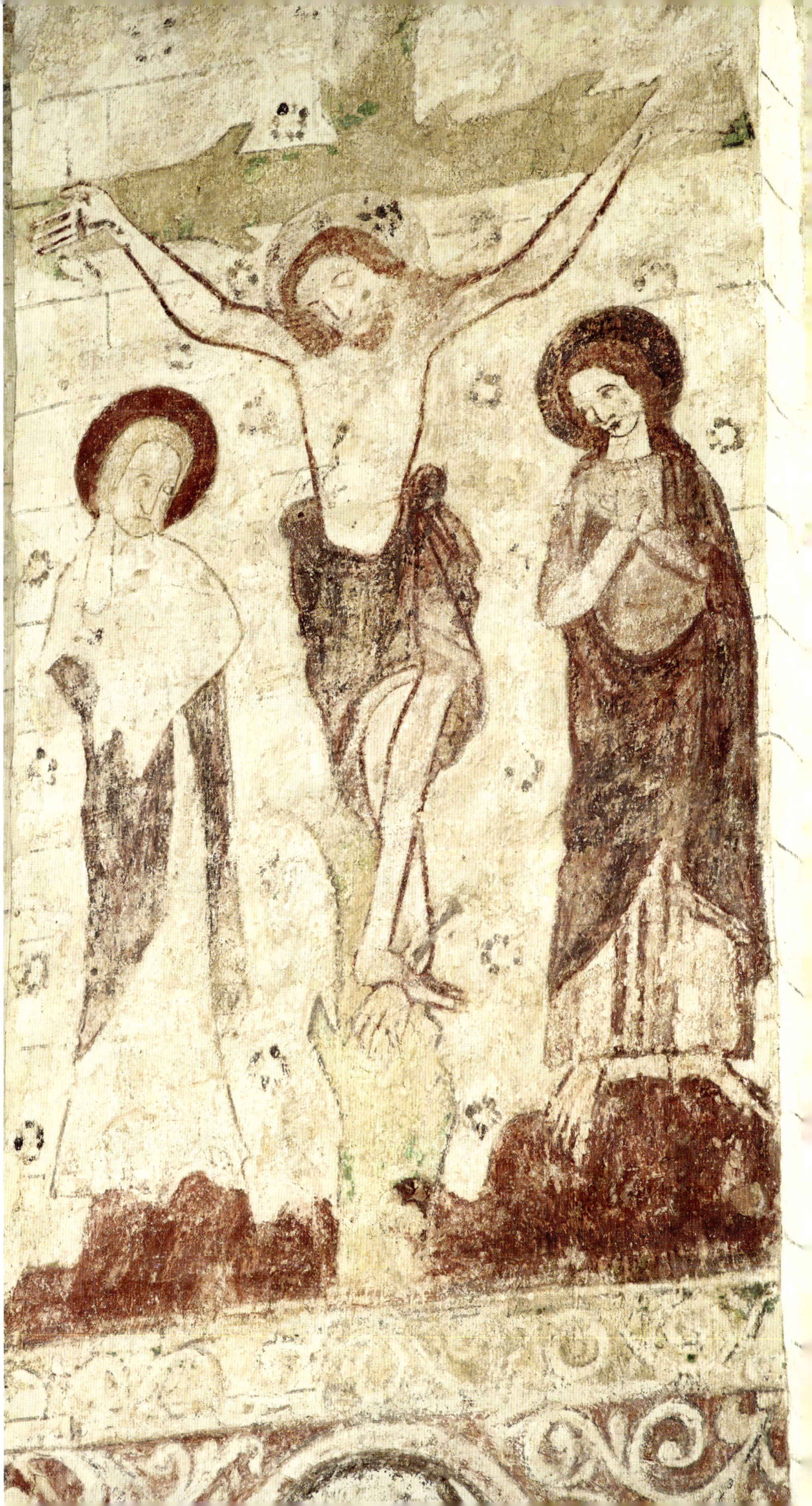

VIRGIN AND CHILD, WITH AN ANGEL(?)

The Virgin sits beneath a five-lobed arch supported on columns with decorated capitals. The squinches (the upper angles formed by the arch) are decorated with stiff-leaf scroll work and the elaborate architectural decoration of the Virgin's throne is still visible. This mural's delicacy of execution contrasts with the robust and more statuesque figure displayed on the first painted pier.

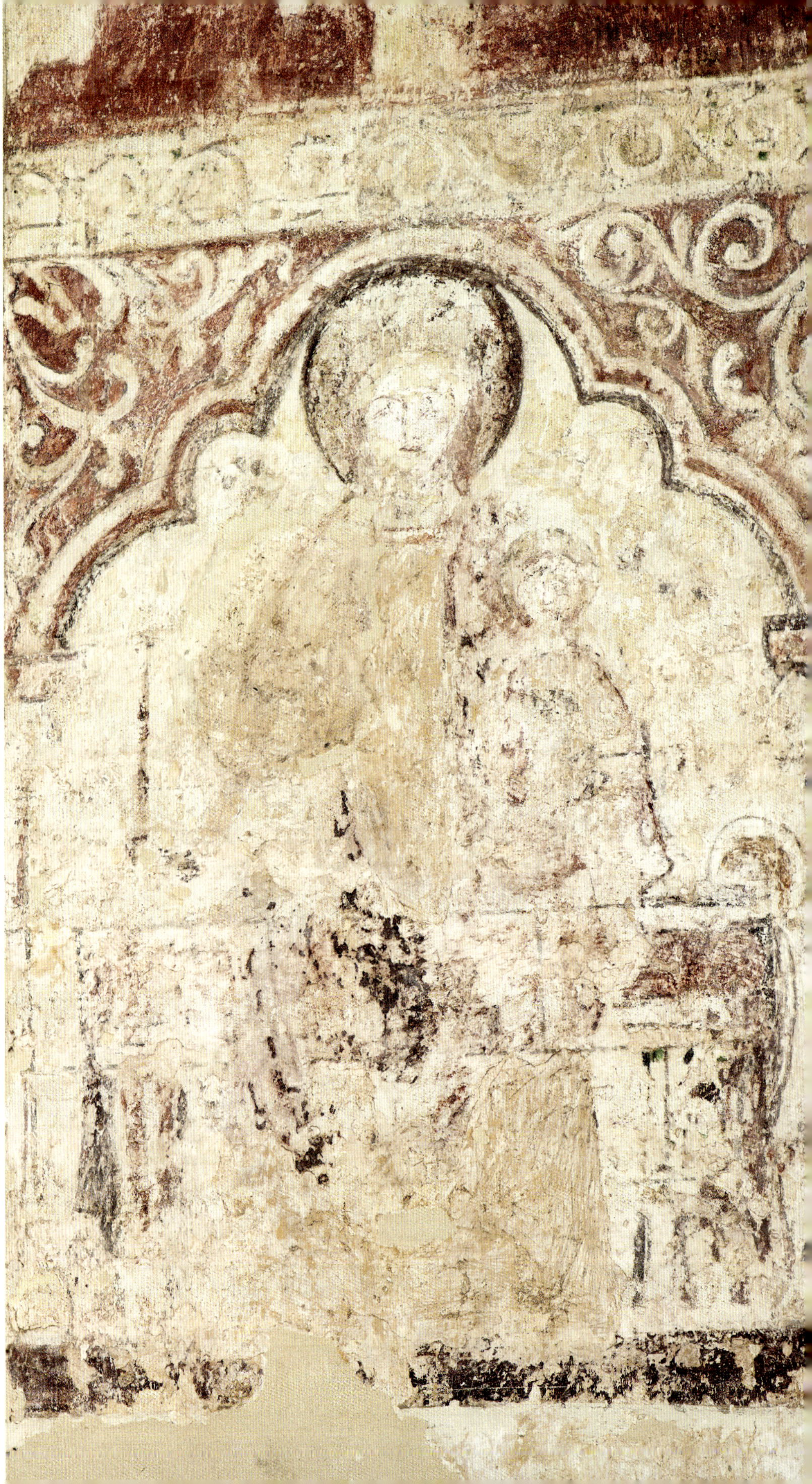

VIRGIN AND CHILD, JOHN OF DALLING'S PSALTER

Monks were required to recite all of the Book of Psalms from the Old Testament every week. Wealthier monks or those in receipt of special patronage would keep highly decorated psalters, invariably containing a calendar with the most important feasts of the so-called 'use' of their monastery, in quires or in chapels, and these often show marks of ownership or commemoration. St Albans was a Benedictine foundation and this psalter (British Library MS Royal 2 B VI, folio 12v.) is one of the few liturgical manuscripts that can be associated directly with the abbey in the thirteenth century. A note at the front of the book records that it was given to St Albans by the monk John of Dalling and that Abbot John of Hertford (1235–60) gave his permission for the book to be used by Dalling during his lifetime. An added note also commemorates the soul of John of Dalling and anathematises anyone who should alienate (remove) the book from the abbey. After the dissolution of the monasteries it was bought by John Theyler (died 1673), a royalist and recusant Catholic. On his son's death, it was bought with part of his library by Charles II and in 1757 was given to the nation by George II.

This image of the Virgin and Child has pride of place in Dalling's psalter and is close iconographically and stylistically to that on the second painted pier. The same artist executed part of the calendar decoration of a psalter that has been associated with Henry III's Queen, Eleanor of Provence (*c.* 1223–91), and her patronage of Fontevrault in Anjou, France, where her daughter, Eleanor of Brittany, became abbess. This suggests that the artists involved in both the wall painting and the illumination of these books were associated with Henry III's court.

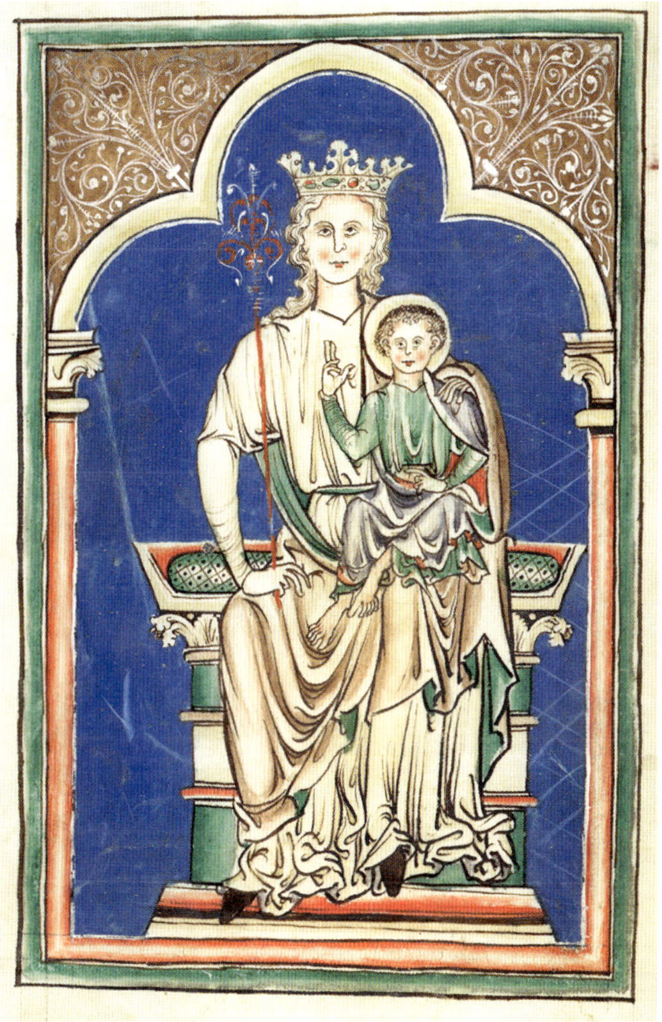

CRUCIFIXION AND ANNUNCIATION

This is the first of the nave pier paintings to abandon the iconography of the frontal, statuesque Virgin and Child below the Crucifixion, instead depicting the Annunciation. This juxtaposition is also frequently found in small devotional ivory carvings of the later thirteenth and fourteenth centuries. The change from the intercessory role of the formal enthroned Virgin to a narrative scene is significant, as it shifts the emphasis of the imagery to the incarnation of Christ and the virginity of Mary. Stylistic changes are also apparent in the handling of the drapery of Christ's *perizonium* (loin cloth) and in the dress of St John and the Virgin, which communicate a formality recalling French and Parisian book illumination of the 1260s–70s. Both the iconography of this pier and its style may be compared with illuminated manuscripts made for patrons in the Midlands, which were probably decorated in Oxford by artists who had migrated there from France.

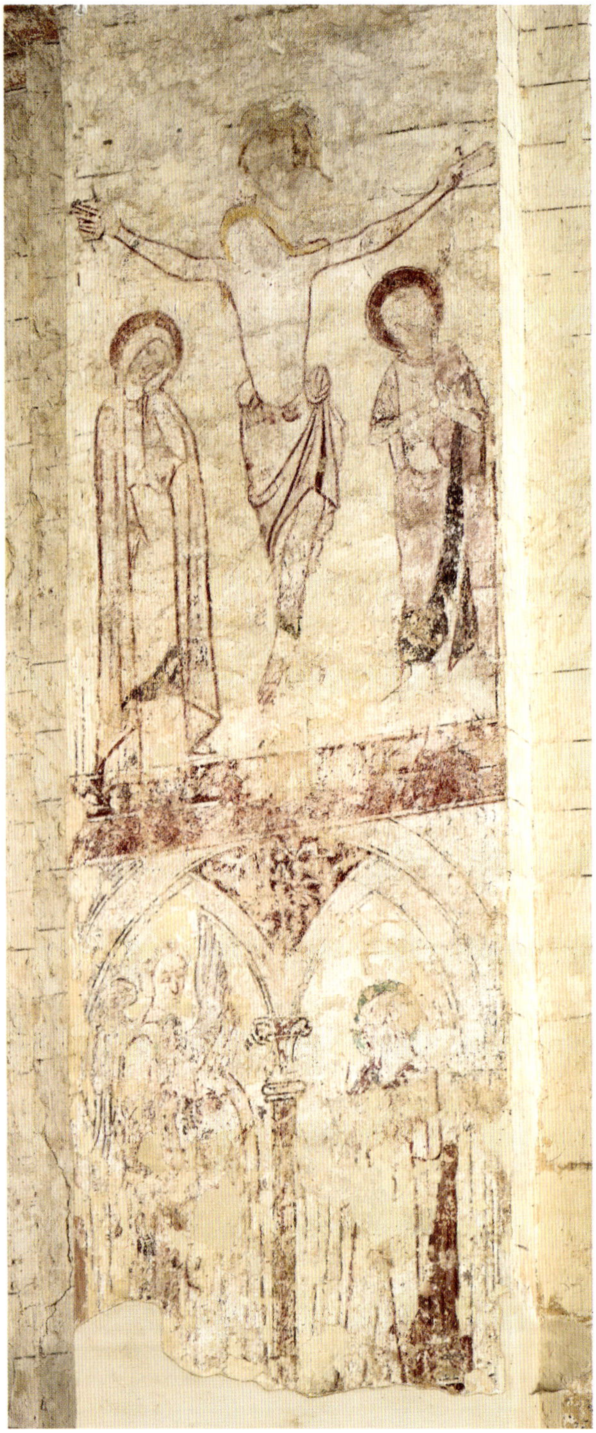

CRUCIFIXION AND VIRGIN AND CHILD, WILLIAM OF DEVON'S BIBLE

This detail of a miniature is from a bible written by a single scribe, who added an endnote or colophon, '*Willelmus Devoniensis scripsit istum librum* ...' (William of Devon wrote this book), ending '... thanks be to the Lord Jesus Christ, and the Blessed Virgin Mary, and all saints, Amen'.[40] Although certainly written in England, *c.* 1260–70, and probably in Oxford, the style and iconography of the book suggest that it was illuminated by artists trained in France, who had probably been attracted to Oxford by the demand for books at the then still relatively new university. The simple angular folds of drapery in the Crucifixion, creating crisp triangular forms, are typical of other surviving illuminated manuscripts executed by the same artists, but the St Albans Crucifixion and Annunciation (see opposite) is the only known wall painting that can be associated with this severe style of painting. The donor is depicted below, praying to St Martin (perhaps his namesake), and the Virgin and Child and the Crucifixion above.

The arrangement of these two scenes recalls that on the first two painted piers of the nave. The Crucifixion itself, between two cherubim, may reflect the arrangement of English rood screens of the thirteenth century, which have been lost.[41] The painted piers of St Albans once faced a rood loft, which was replaced by the current stone screen in the fourteenth century. Although this is a common devotional theme in itself, some reference to the rood loft may have been intended in the repetition of Crucifixion scenes on the piers.

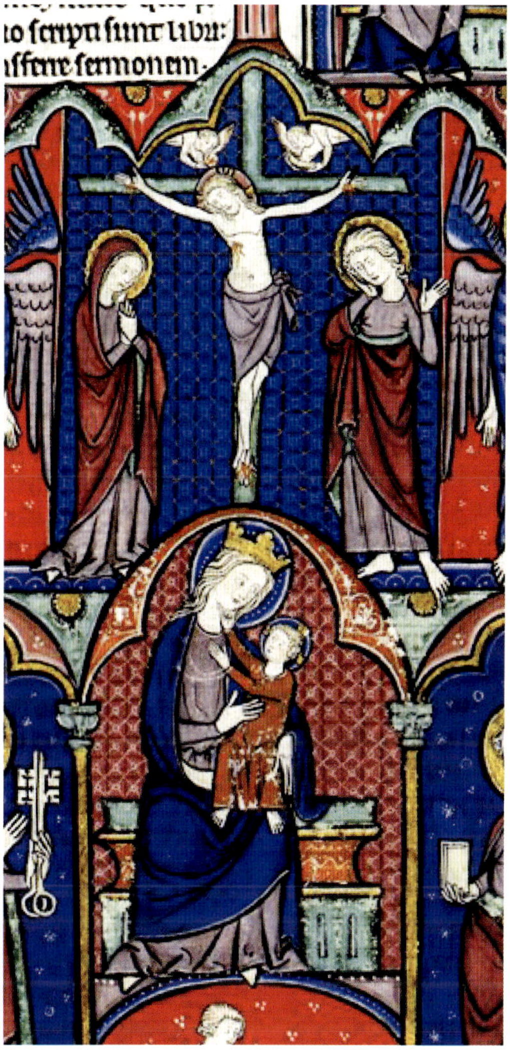

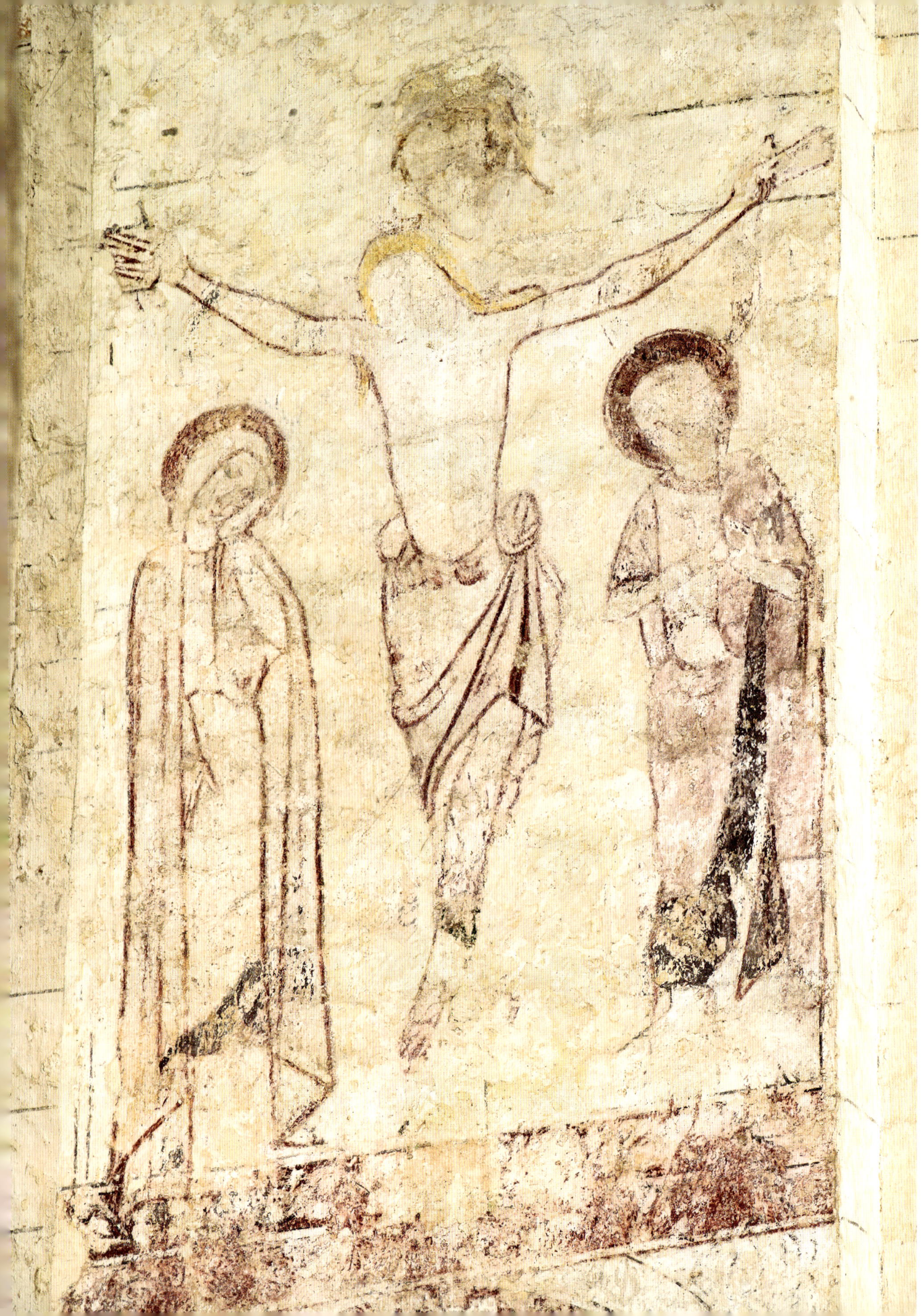

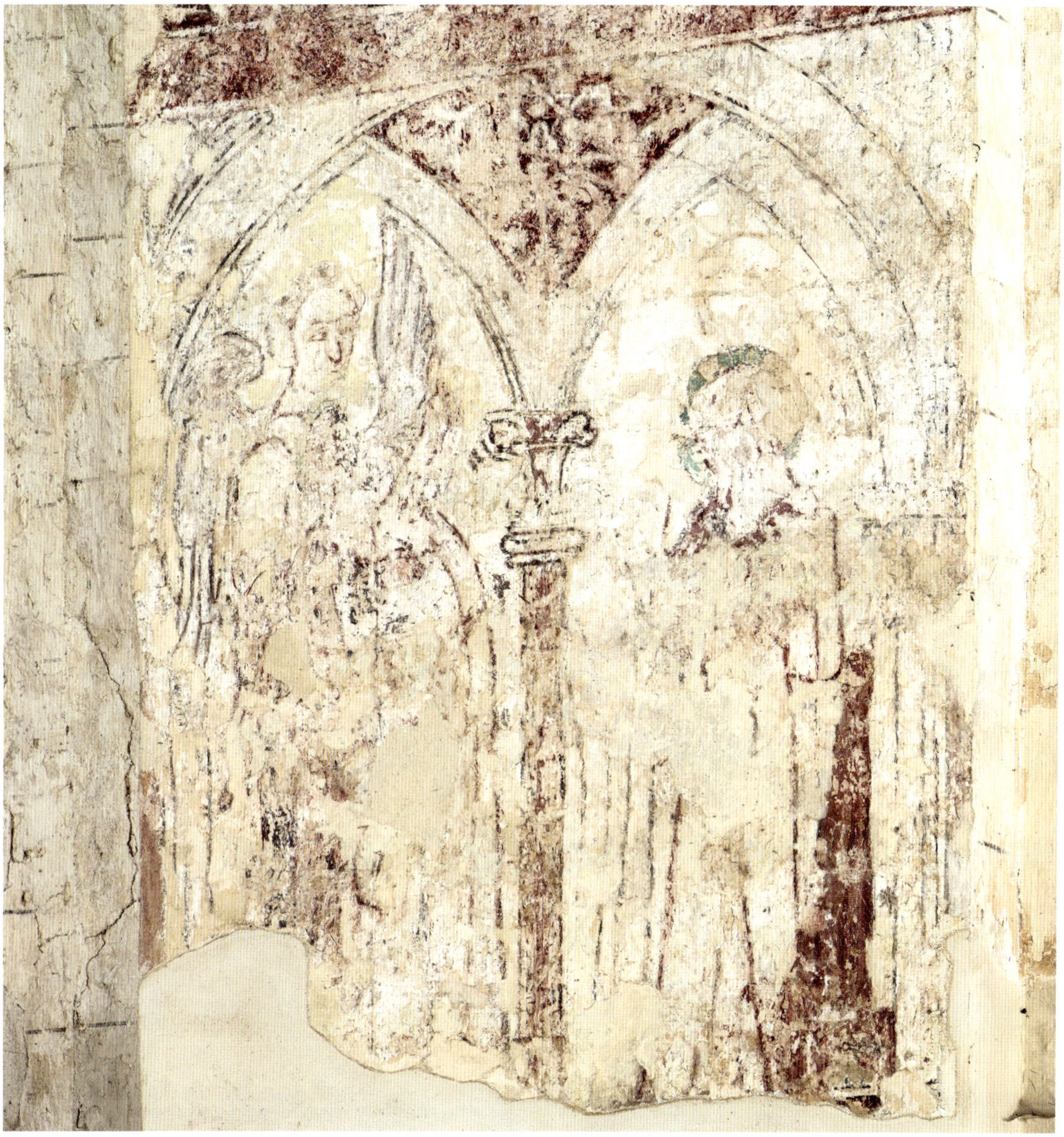

CRUCIFIXION

Comparison between Christ's *perizonium* (loin cloth) and that in the Crucifixion in William of Devon's bible shows that a similar model has been used for the outline, suggesting a close stylistic connection between the artists.

ANNUNCIATION

The Oscott Psalter (*c.* 1265–70) displays a similar arrangement to this, where the angel of the Annunciation is separated from the Virgin by a column.[42] Repair work behind the head of the Virgin gives the impression that another taller figure or a curtain may once have occupied the space behind her.

CRUCIFIXION AND ANNUNCIATION

The theme of the iconography here follows that of the previous pier, with the Crucifixion above the Annunciation, but the approach to the two scenes is very different. Although the image is badly damaged, the rendering of the body of Christ marks a new departure in the depiction of the Crucifixion at St Albans. Emphasis is placed on the awkward angularity of the body, suggesting pain. Christ's right arm is depicted almost parallel with the beam of the cross, while his left arm is in a subtly more attenuated position, reacting to the weight of the body which shifts to the right as the head dips on the left. Marks on the lower legs suggest injury or blood and his loin cloth or *perizonium* is no longer presented frontally but hangs freely on the right. This emphasis on the suffering of Christ can be paralleled in illuminated manuscripts such as the Evesham Psalter, perhaps made for Abbot Henry of Worcester (*c.*1250–60),[43] but the movement in the body suggests a later date than this. If the Annunciation below was painted at the same time as the Crucifixion, which seems likely, this suggests a date of *c.* 1300 or later. The elongated bodies of the angel and the Virgin present two highly stylised figures, which may be compared in wall painting with the much grander figure of St Faith at Westminster Abbey (after 1303?).[44]

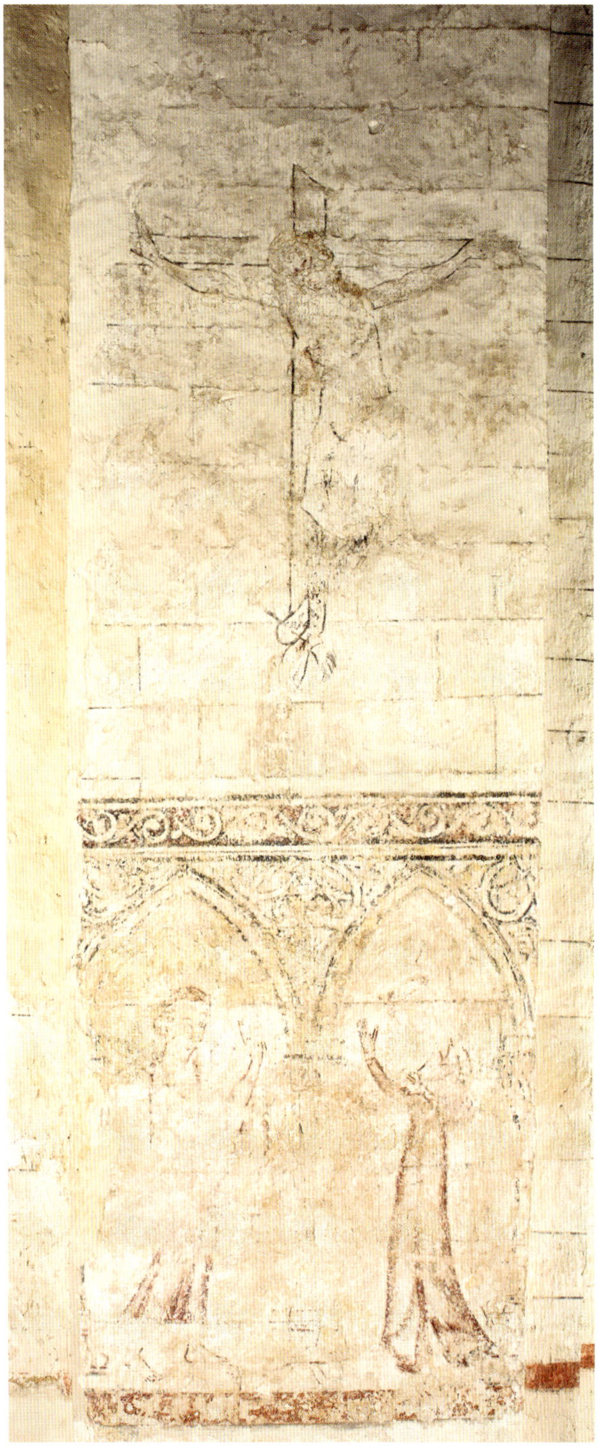

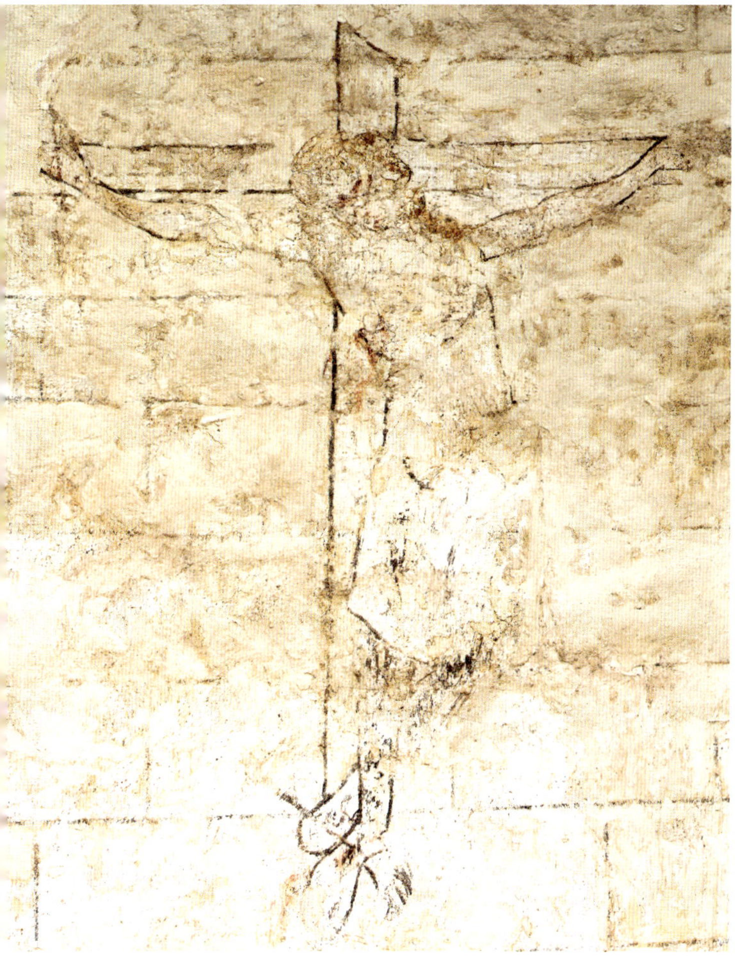

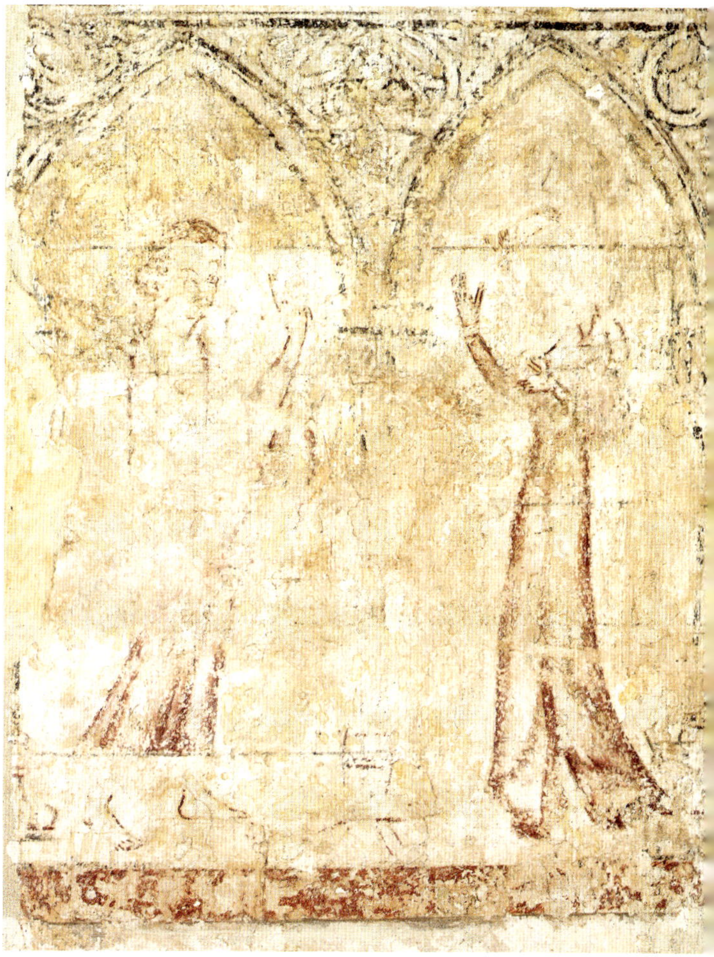

CRUCIFIXION

When compared with the first painted pier of *c.* 1190 –1220, the developing emphasis on the suffering of Christ can be seen clearly in this image. This is evidence of how such images effected changes in the way people engaged with prayer.

ANNUNCIATION

The double-arched frame providing canopies for the angel and the Virgin reflects the composition of the previous pier, but here the column that separates the two has been removed to suggest a unified space.

PAINTED NAVE PIER 5 WEST FACE CRUCIFIXION AND CORONATION OF THE VIRGIN

CRUCIFIXION AND CORONATION OF THE VIRGIN

The fifth painted pier is made up of segments of a circular shaft with flat facets at each corner. As in many of the great Romanesque churches in England, this extra architectural (and often sculptural) decoration designated a space close to a nave altar. Paintings were placed all over the available surfaces, whether curved or not, and traces of another Crucifixion shown above a seated figure – almost certainly the Virgin and Child – and other evidence of painting can still be detected on the south faces of the pier.

On the eastern inner face of the pier the Crucifixion above is here accompanied by a Coronation of the Virgin with censing angels. It takes the theme of the suffering of Christ one step further by showing the head and body of Christ leaning forwards towards the viewer, while the Virgin and St John stand on rocky outcrops which fill the space left by the tri-lobed frame of the Coronation of the Virgin below. The doubled-up body of Christ and the treatment of the feet may be compared with illuminated manuscripts produced in the period *c.*1290–1320, such as the Ramsey Abbey Psalter made for Abbot John of Sawtry (1285–1316) probably as a gift from his cellarer, William of Grafham (1303–10).[45] The Coronation of the Virgin with censing angels is also close in composition to that of the Ramsey Psalter. It reflects the increasing popularity of regal imagery associated with the Virgin in the later fourteenth century; many small devotional ivory carvings depict a similar scene. It is significant that this painting may date to the abbacy of Hugh of Eversden (1308–28), when the Lady Chapel at the east end of St Albans was finally completed.

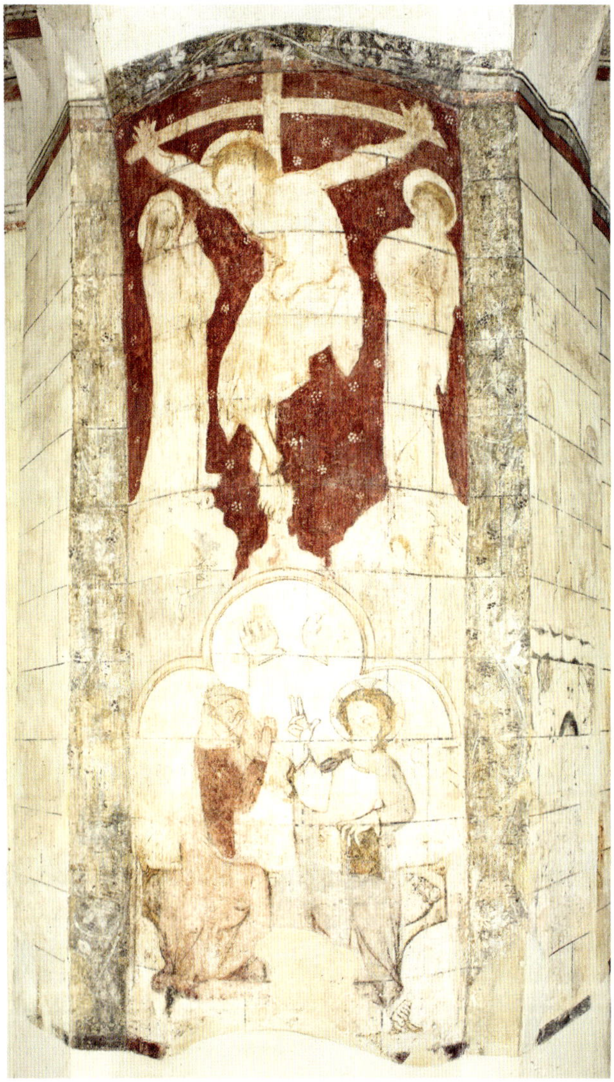

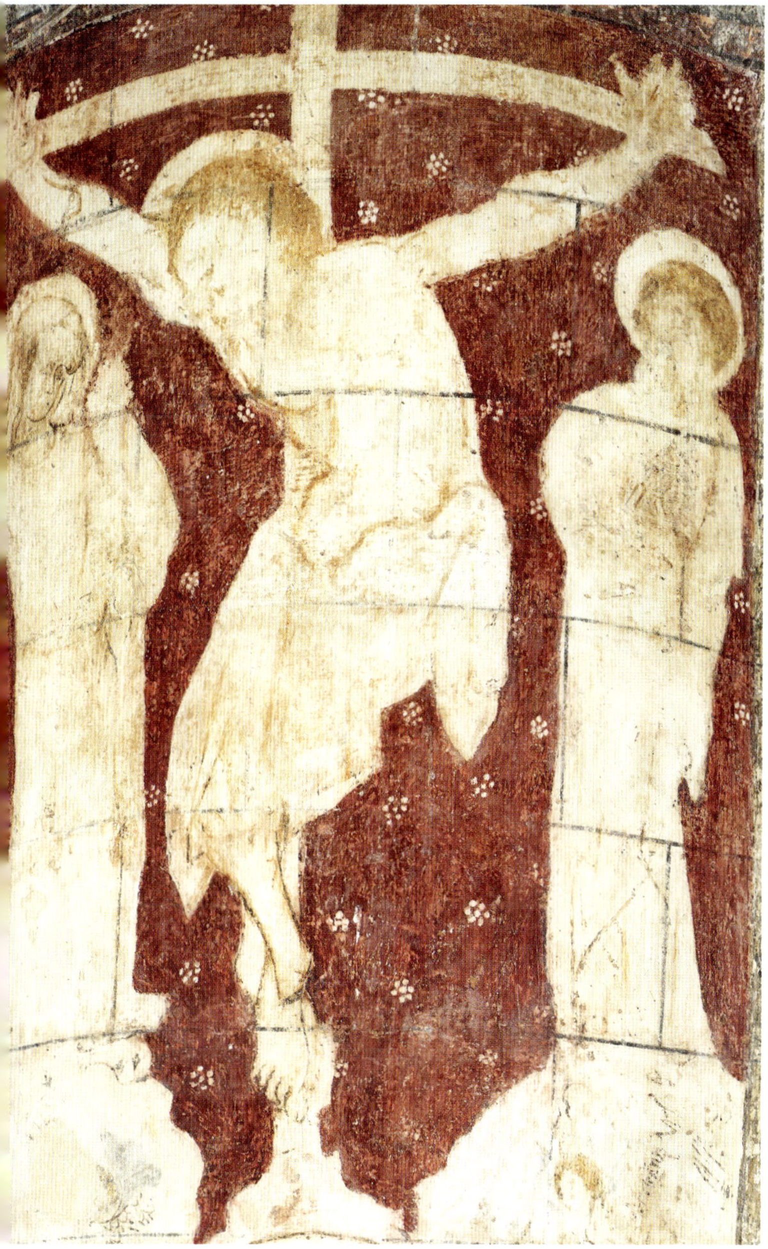

CRUCIFIXION

The unusual depiction of the Virgin and St John on mounds of earth may reflect the presence of the rood loft at St Albans before the collapse of the south nave aisle in 1323. The *Triumphkreuzgruppe* (rood cross group) on the screen at Halberstadt Cathedral, Saxony (1215–20), shows a similar arrangement that may reflect lost examples in England.

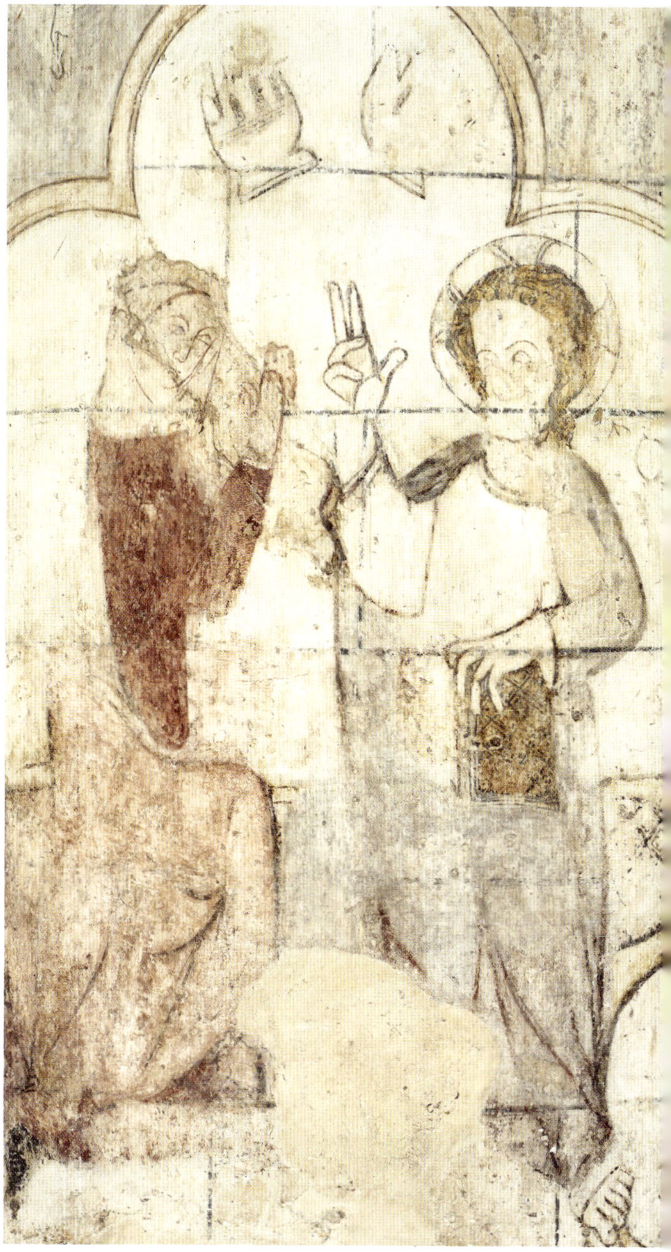

CORONATION OF THE VIRGIN

It was common in England for the Coronation of the Virgin to be represented as Christ shown blessing his mother. In the rest of Europe, whether in ivory carving, monumental sculpture, mosaics or painting, the crown is more often shown being placed on her head by an angel or by Christ himself.

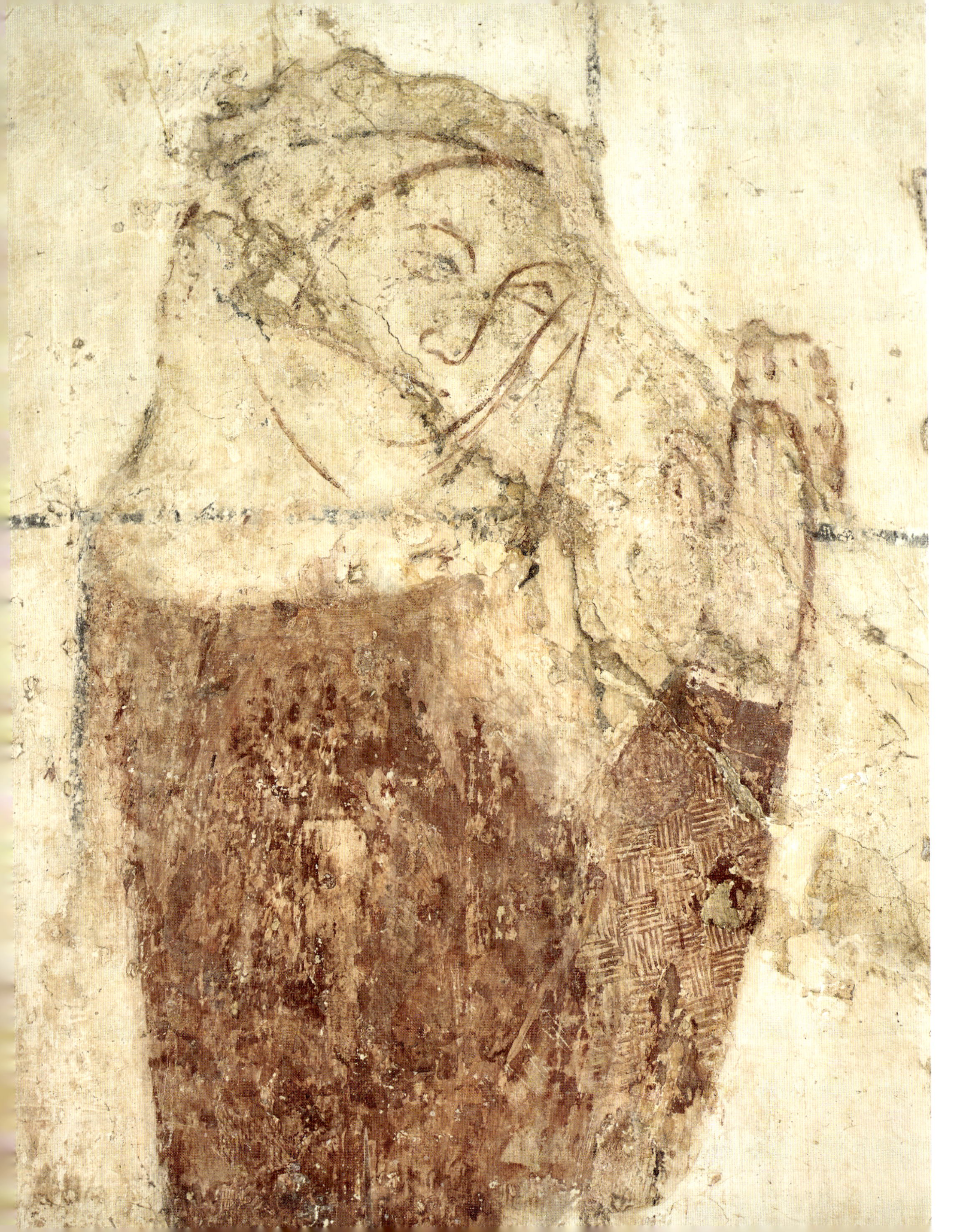

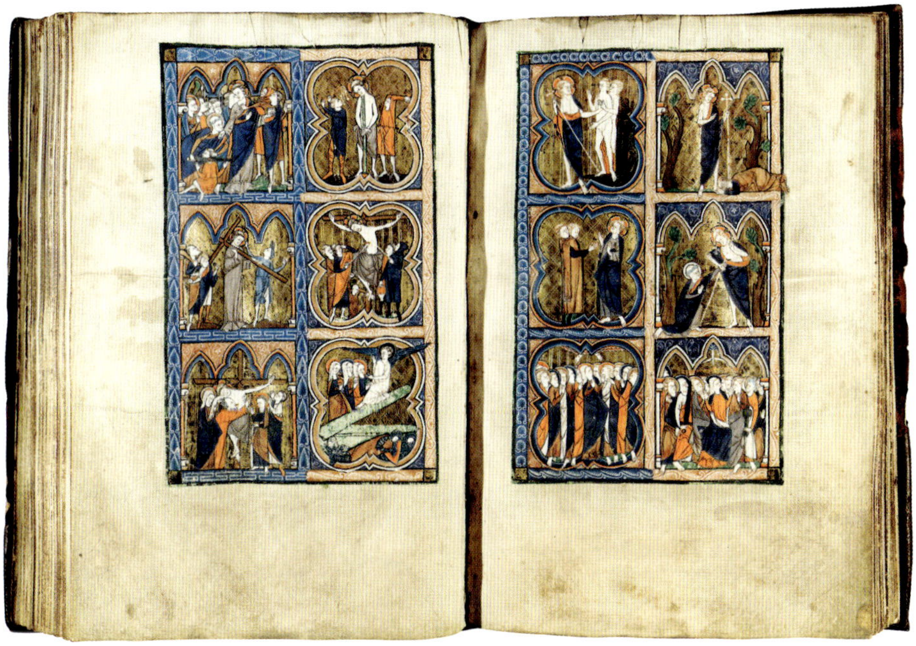

PASSION AND RESURRECTION SCENES, PSALTER OF WILLIAM CLARKSON

This beautifully illuminated psalter (Cambridge, Trinity, MS 0 4 16) belongs to a group of manuscripts which have been associated with patronage at the court of Edward I. A sixteenth-century inscription added to an inserted miniature of the mid-fifteenth century states: 'Of your charyte pray for the soull of Wyllyam Clarkson ferrar [farrier] of London and Margaret hys wyffe and all [th]ere childaris.' An unusually close comparison can be made between the faces in the scene of the Coronation of the Virgin and those in the miniatures added to the psalter (folios 113v–114r). The style of drawing in the psalter is closely related to that of the so-called Windmill Psalter (which may have been made for Edward I) and of the Bible paraphrase known as the *Historia Scholastica* of Petrus Comestor, a copy of which was given by Edmund, Earl of Cornwall, (died 1300) to his foundation at Ashridge Priory, Bucks.[46] The Coronation of the Virgin on the fifth painted pier is considerably different in style from the Crucifixion and much closer to that of the Clarkson psalter, suggesting that the two paintings may date from slightly different periods or have been executed by two different artists working together, *c.* 1290–1310.

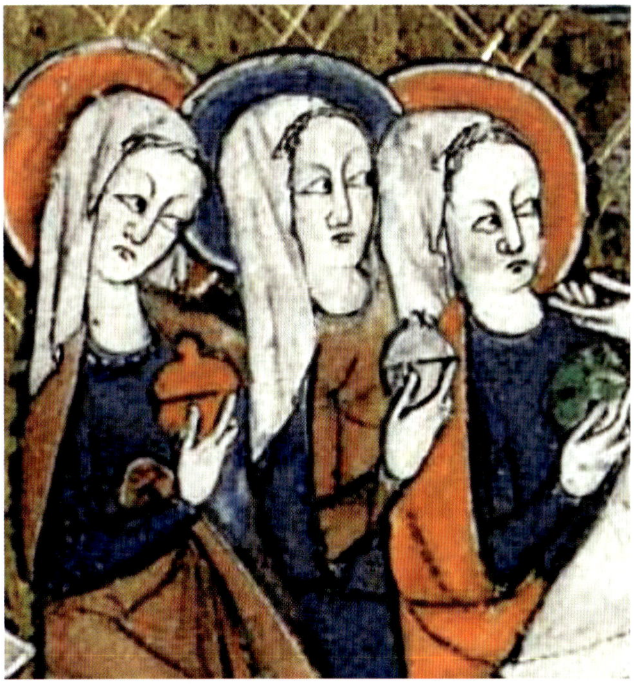

VIRGIN FROM THE CORONATION OF THE VIRGIN *(opposite)*
THREE MARYS FROM THE CLARKSON PSALTER *(left)*

The elegant facial structure of both the Virgin and the Three Marys at the Tomb of Christ in the Clarkson psalter suggests a close relationship between the two. Although there are some exceptions, wall paintings in parish churches rarely bear such close comparison with miniatures. Here, as in the case of the William of Devon group of illuminators who can be associated with the third painted pier, the resemblance suggests a common training, which may reflect the close connections that St Albans maintained with the court during the reigns of Henry III and Edward I.

THRONE OF GRACE TRINITY (?)

The very faded painting on this pier was recorded by John Carter in 1813 in a drawing for the Society of Antiquaries; he interpreted it as a figure of Christ with outstretched arms, above, and St Elizabeth and the Virgin in the scene of the Visitation, below.[47] In 1882 Ridgway Lloyd believed he could decipher the Greek letters '*XPE* [signifying Christ] ... *Amen* ... *Sanct[us]*', but what can be seen is more likely to be a request invoking the Trinity, with the words '... *tuum sa[nctum]*' still visible on the left-hand side. The words on the right are as yet indecipherable although the letters '*go*', perhaps for '*rogo*' (I request) can be seen.[48] Given the previous pier's iconographical theme, it is highly unlikely that the Visitation would have been depicted, and there is no evidence of a division of scenes between the remaining head of Christ above and the lower part of the pier and its inscriptions. A depiction of the *Gnadenstuhl*, the Throne of Grace Trinity, is visible on the second pier after the nave screen (see opposite), which was unknown to Carter but was recorded by Lloyd in 1883, and it is likely that this is what was depicted here.

The Throne of Grace Trinity was a popular symbol in the early fourteenth century, depicting God the Father supporting the cross of Christ with the Holy Spirit descending in the form of a dove. The two figures that were at one time visible on the lower part of the painting were probably donors, who would be associated with prayers rising from the scrolls which they would have held. The imitation stonework which has survived forms part of the original painting of all the painted piers (save the first), to which the surviving paintings were progressively added during the thirteenth and fourteenth centuries.

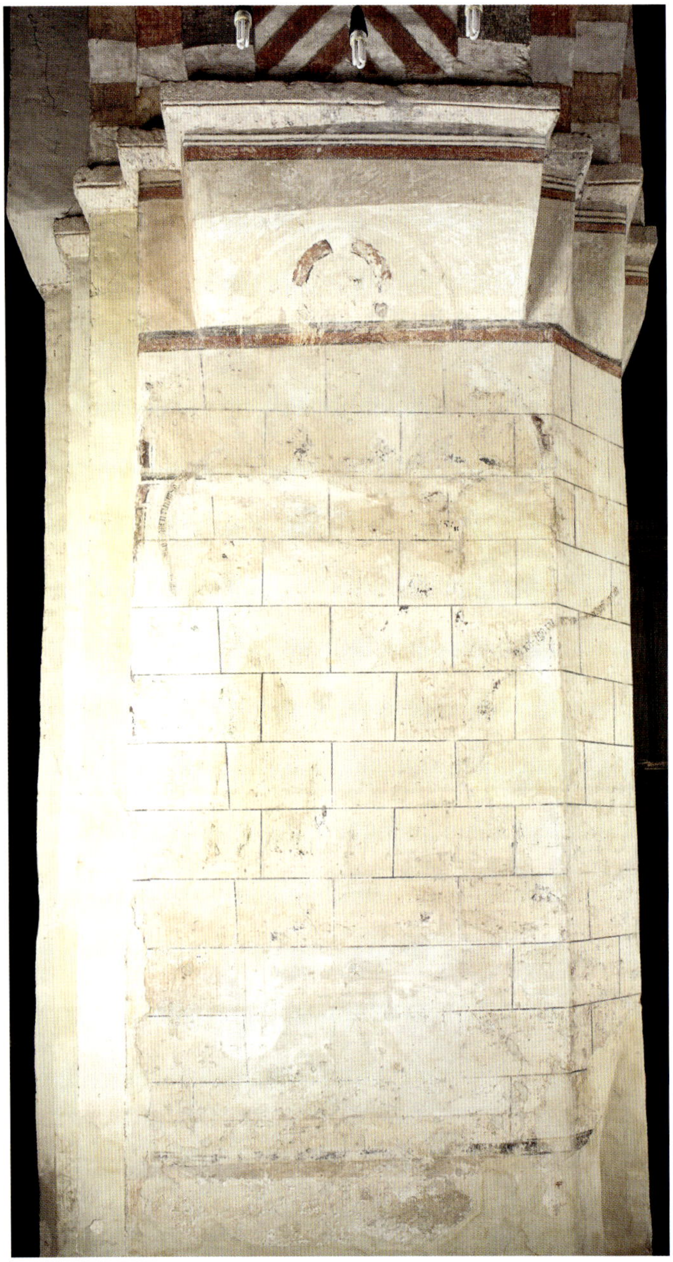

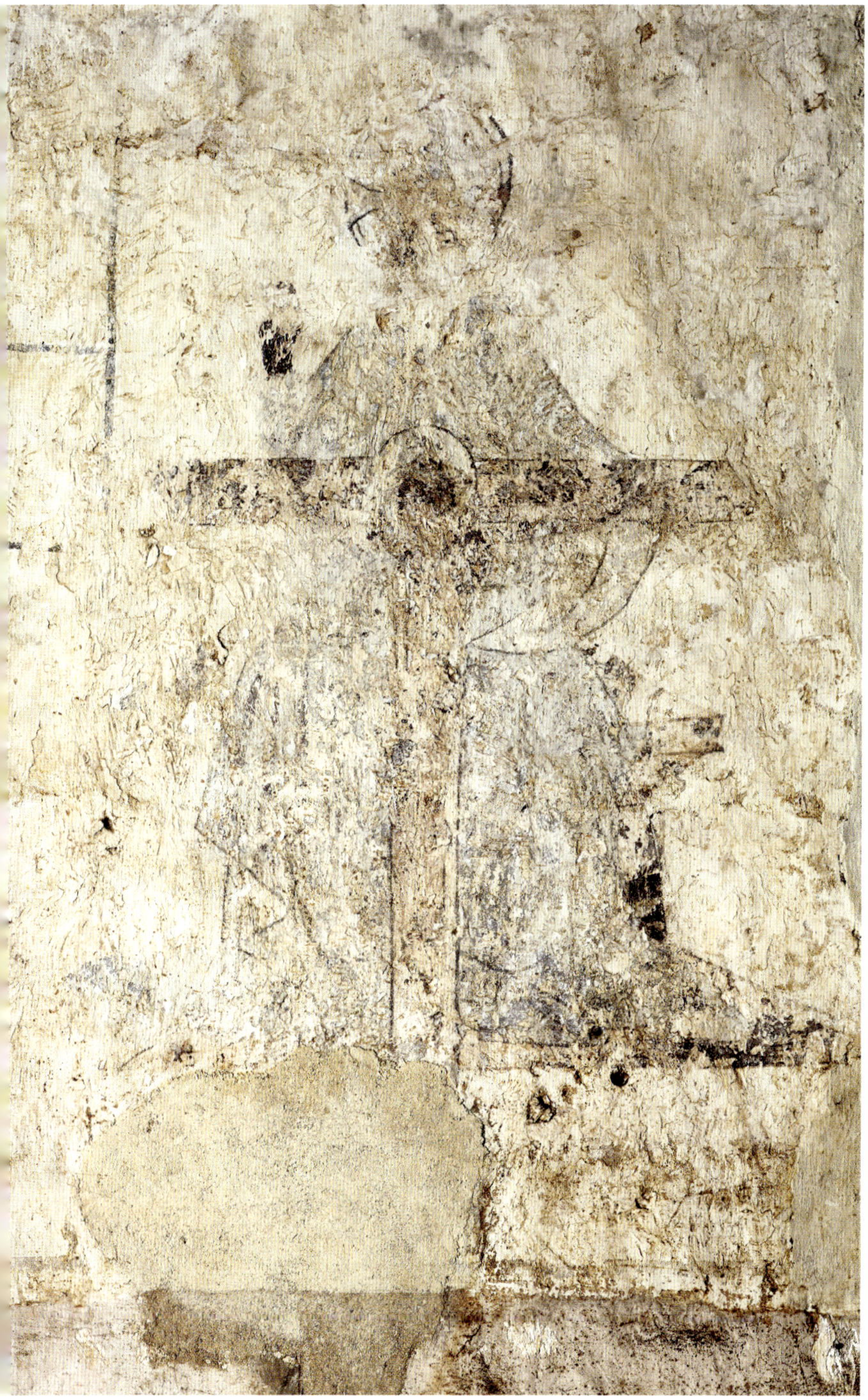

THRONE OF GRACE TRINITY

The painted piers, once thought to be exclusive to the nave, in fact continued beyond the nave screen – evidence of this can be detected on at least two. This indicates that before the stone nave screen replaced the earlier rood screen (damaged in the collapse of the south nave piers in 1323), a more unified decorative scheme existed and was probably completed before the stone screen was erected. The scene that has survived represents the *Gnadenstuhl* or Throne of Grace Trinity, an iconography that was particularly popular in the late thirteenth and fourteenth centuries as a devotional focus.

The recent discovery of a wall painting depicting a similar scene at St Mary's church, Houghton-on-the-Hill, Norfolk, dated to *c.* 1100–25, has led to the theory that this was an Anglo-Saxon development, but contemporary examples in other countries suggest it was promulgated all over Europe for theological reasons.[49] The controversy over whether the Holy Spirit flowed from both the Father and the Son (*filioque*) came to a head in the eleventh century, when the Eastern Church rejected this term. The creation of this Trinitarian iconography in the West, with the inclusion of the dove at its centre, appears to give visual expression to the idea of the Holy Spirit flowing from both Father and Son. Some of the earliest examples of the Throne of Grace Trinity are found in a missal (used for the celebration of the mass) and on a portable altar of the early twelfth century, suggesting that the image was originally directly linked to the celebration of the mass.[50] It provides a link between Christ's sacrifice and the redemption of mankind. The fact that God holds up his son's body so that atonement for sin and redemption can be achieved through prayer made it a particularly popular image in a variety of media.

ST CHRISTOPHER

St Christopher, holding the cross-nimbed Christ Child on his left shoulder, stands beneath an ogee arch. The arch's central finial and side pinnacles are still visible at the top, and an inscription may once have run across behind his head. The earliest image in English art of St Christopher with the Christ Child is found in the Westminster Psalter of *c.* 1250.[51] His popularity was spread by his story's inclusion in *The Golden Legend*, a popular collection of saints' lives by Jacobus da Voragine (*c.* 1230–98). By the end of the fourteenth century most English parish churches had Christopher images, often painted on the north wall opposite the entrance so that they would be seen on entering the church. Although Christopher is now thought of as a patron of travellers, before the Reformation his image itself was believed to afford protection against sudden death. A scroll or inscription (still visible here to the left of the figure) would often be displayed, stating that whoever saw the image would not die that day. Christopher's strength was also invoked and popular prayers to St Christopher addressed him as *'bonus athleta Christoforus'* (wonderful athlete Christopher).

Although many images of St Christopher have survived on the walls of English parish churches, the composition here recalls that of a psalter adapted for use at Peterborough Abbey *c.* 1320, where he accompanies the Virgin and Child. Part of his flowering staff (Christ tells him to plant it in the ground for it to bear leaves) is visible in his hand on the left-hand side as he wades through water. He is the only saint, other than the Virgin, who had the privilege of bearing the Christ Child on his arm.[52]

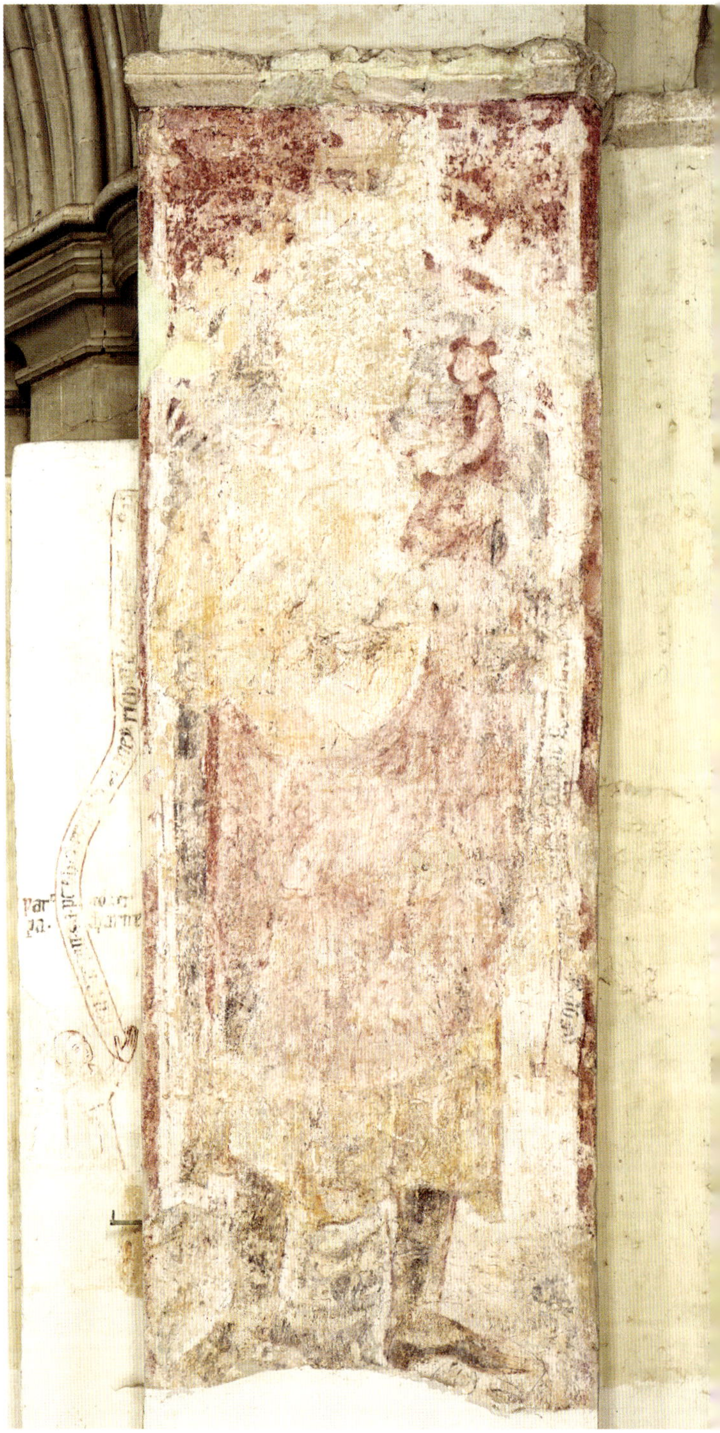

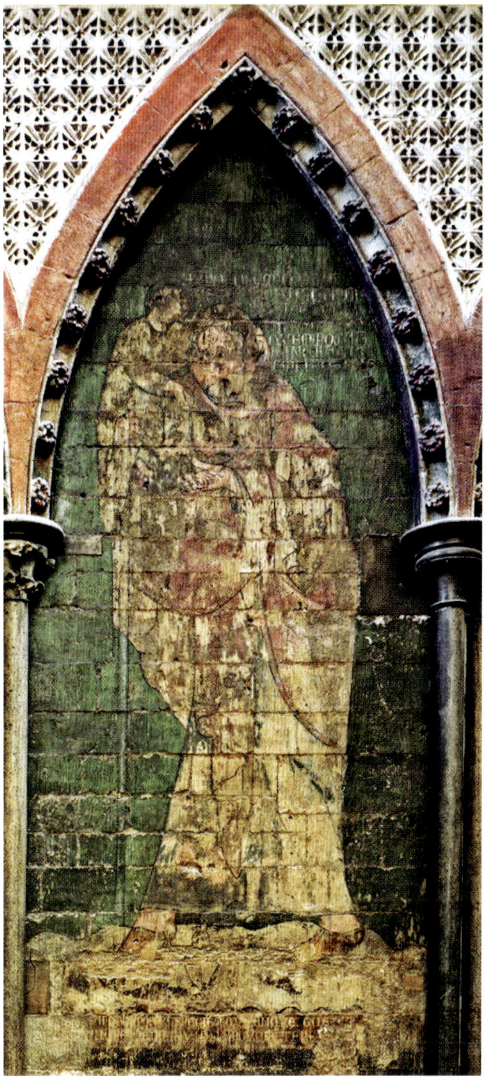

ST CHRISTOPHER, WESTMINSTER ABBEY

The earliest references to images of the saint are found in the records of paintings carried out for Henry III at St Peter ad Vincula in the Tower of London, where he ordered: 'an image of Saint Christopher holding and carrying Jesus... to be made and painted where it may best and most suitably be placed' (1240). Another image of the saint 'as he is painted elsewhere' was made for the chapel of Queen Eleanor of Provence (1236–72) at Winchester Castle (1248).[53] This wall painting from the south transept of Westminster Abbey (1270) carries the inscription, often associated with such images, *'Sancti Christophori speciem quicumque tuetur / Illa nempe die languore tenetur'* (whoever sees Saint Christopher this day is protected, nor seized by illness).

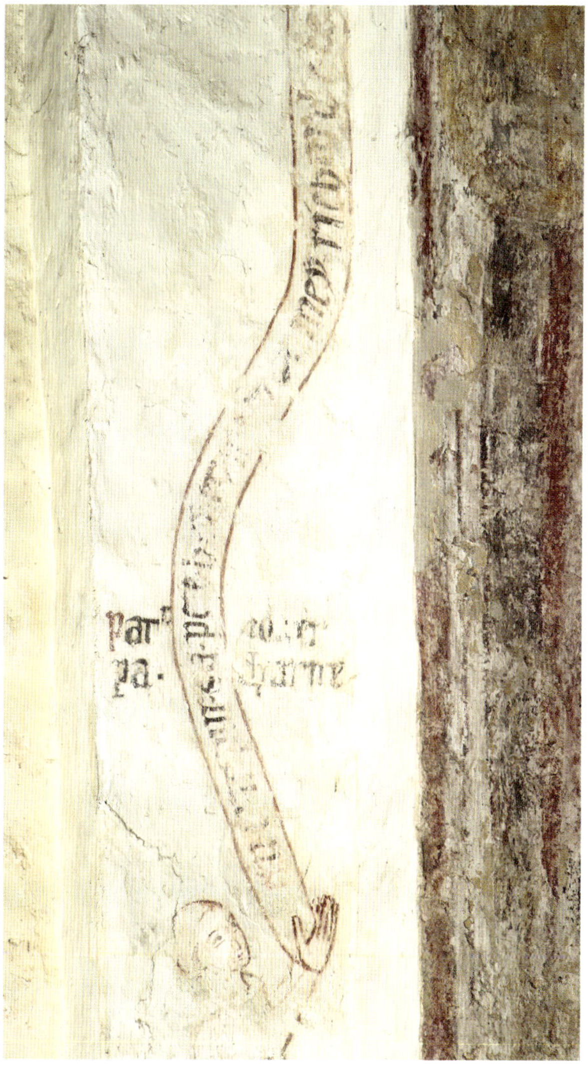

DONOR FIGURE 'DOMINEY RICHARD'

Part of the inscription on the scroll carried by the diminutive figure who looks up at St Christopher on the inner left moulding of the pier has been recently read as 'Dominey Richard' (Lord Richard).[54] The title 'Dominey' suggests that this is Abbot Richard of Wallingford (1292–1336), the maker of the great St Albans clock.[55] The heavily abbreviated words of what may be the *Pater Noster* (Lord's Prayer) run across the inscription, one of several for which evidence has survived in the nave recording lay as well as monastic gifts to fund the painting and repainting of the piers.

ST THOMAS BECKET

Since Becket's altar is recorded as '*coram sancta cruce ... situata*' (placed against the rood screen), this image was therefore within sight of the altar.[56] Becket, clothed in full mass vestments, stands beneath a cusped ogee arch, with a cartouche running behind his defaced head still bearing the letters '*S*', '*M*(?)' and '*AS*' for *'Sanctus Martyr(?) Thomas'*. He wears episcopal gloves and blesses with his right hand. The archbishop's cross staff or crozier is in his left hand and a maniple is draped over his arm, its wide terminal and full fringe still distinctly visible. He stands on a jewelled pedestal and wears an alb, over which hangs the bottom of a dalmatic, a long tunic. His arms emerge from an outer vestment, the chasuble, over which the white band of an archbishop's pallium can be seen at the centre and on his right shoulder. The small crosses that would have decorated the pallium and the orphrey (the ornamental border on the hem of his alb) now appear as darkened areas.

The deliberate diagonal cuts into the plaster (seen on the other figures to a somewhat lesser extent) indicate vehement defacement. Henry VIII's proclamation of November 1538 stated that: 'Thomas Becket, sometime archbishop of Canterbury, shall no longer be named a saint ... His pictures throughout the realm are to be plucked down and his festival shall no longer be kept, and the services in his name shall be razed out of all books.' Nevertheless this is the largest such image to have survived in England, rivalling in size the great stained-glass window at Canterbury, which avoided the initial cull only to be smashed in 1643 during the Commonwealth.

At bottom right, traces of paint where a kneeling donor figure would normally have been placed can just be made out. The head of another small figure was also added, facing towards St Thomas on one of the stepped mouldings of the arch on the left. This is in keeping with the evidence from the St Christopher figure on p. 40, which has a donor figure placed on the left, and the inscription beneath the images of Sts Alban and Amphibalus on the fourth painted pier. It is further evidence that individual donors gave money for the painting, upkeep or repainting of these images.

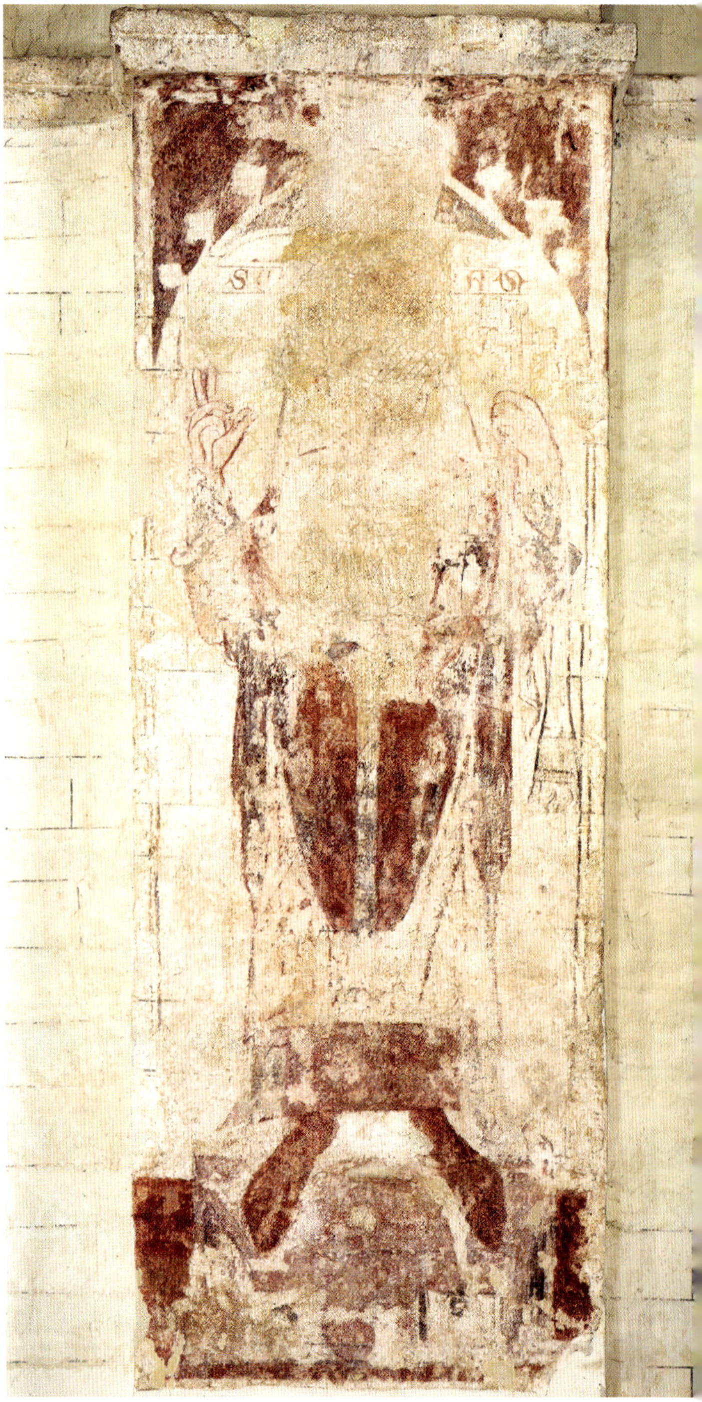

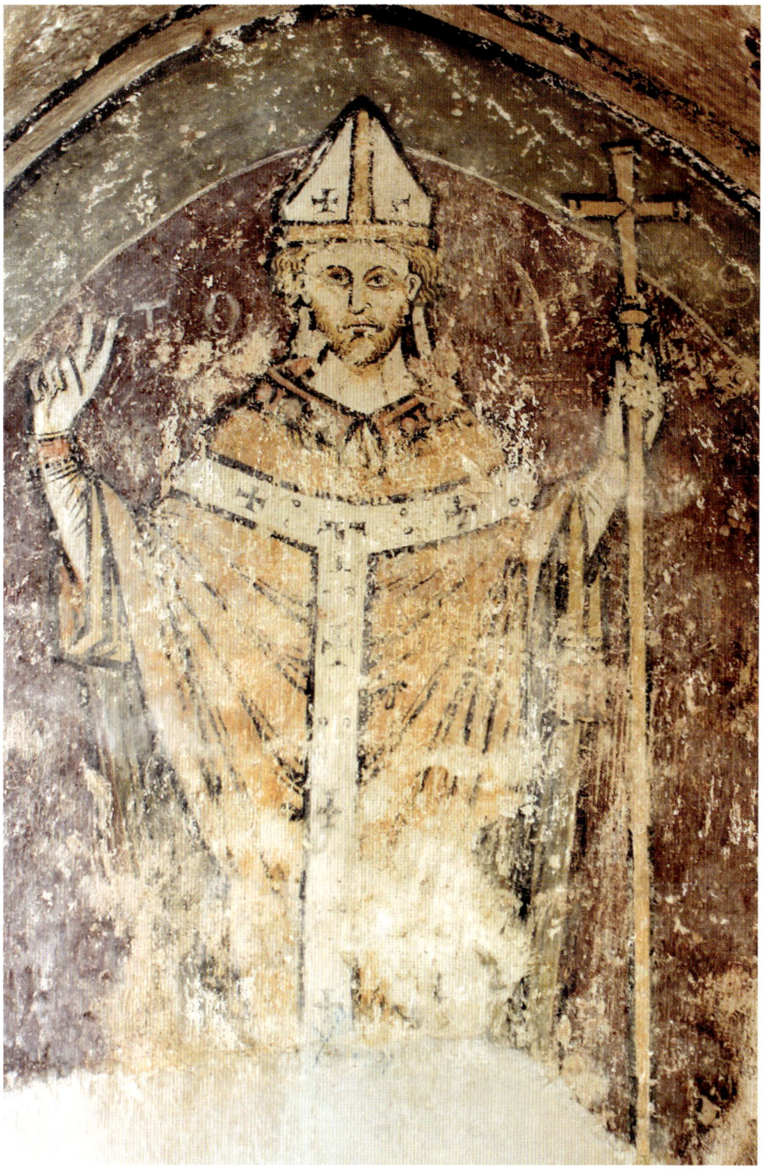

ST THOMAS BECKET, HAUXTON, CAMBRIDGESHIRE

This late thirteenth-century painting was walled up before the dissolution of the monasteries and the anathematisation of Becket by Henry VIII, and so has survived defacement. It presents Becket in the same pose as that depicted at St Albans, wearing mass vestments and raising his right hand in blessing. The inscription again runs behind the head of the saint, but here he retains his mitre and his face is unscathed. Although the lower half of the figure has disappeared, the apparels (decoration) to his collar-like amice can be seen below his neck, as can the crosses that decorate his pallium.

PAINTED NAVE PIER 3 SOUTH FACE
ST SITHA OF LUCCA

ST SITHA OF LUCCA

The tall figure of St Sitha, much mutilated around the face, stands beneath a cusped ogee arch that has central finial and side pinnacles of the same design as those above St Christopher and St Thomas Becket. This suggests that all three were painted, probably in sequence, over a short period of time in the fourteenth century. On the right-hand side the remains of a cartouche can be seen which would have run behind her head, the letters '*S*' and '*C*' (for *Sancta Sitha*) still visible.[57] According to Amundesham's account of the altars, written in *c.* 1428, St Sitha's altar was placed in the north transept on the south-east wall beneath the window nearest the crossing.[58] The positioning of her image in the nave fits in with the emphasis on the 'edification of lay people' which Abbot William of Trumpington referred to when he reordered and replaced the sculpture on the nave screen.[59]

St Sitha (died 1272) was a maidservant who worked for the Fatinelli family of Lucca in Italy. Her story was quickly transmitted back to England through texts that were copied at Bury St Edmunds in the thirteenth century. By the end of the fourteenth century she had become one of the most popular saints in England and in the fifteenth century the story of her life was translated into English.[60] She appealed particularly to women and servants because of her acts of kindness, her resistance to the advances of men and the instructions of her master Pagano di Guglielmo. From the employer's point of view, she promoted diligence and work. Other servants, jealous of her hard-working nature, are said to have reported her for giving bread to the poor, against Pagano's wishes, but when she was confronted the bread had miraculously become a bunch of flowers. She is shown here holding up another of her attributes, a rosary, but a circular object just visible in her hands may well be a loaf of bread or a garland of flowers. A purse and keys are often shown in Sitha images, and the indistinct rhomboid shapes that have survived below her waist may represent a purse hanging from a belt.

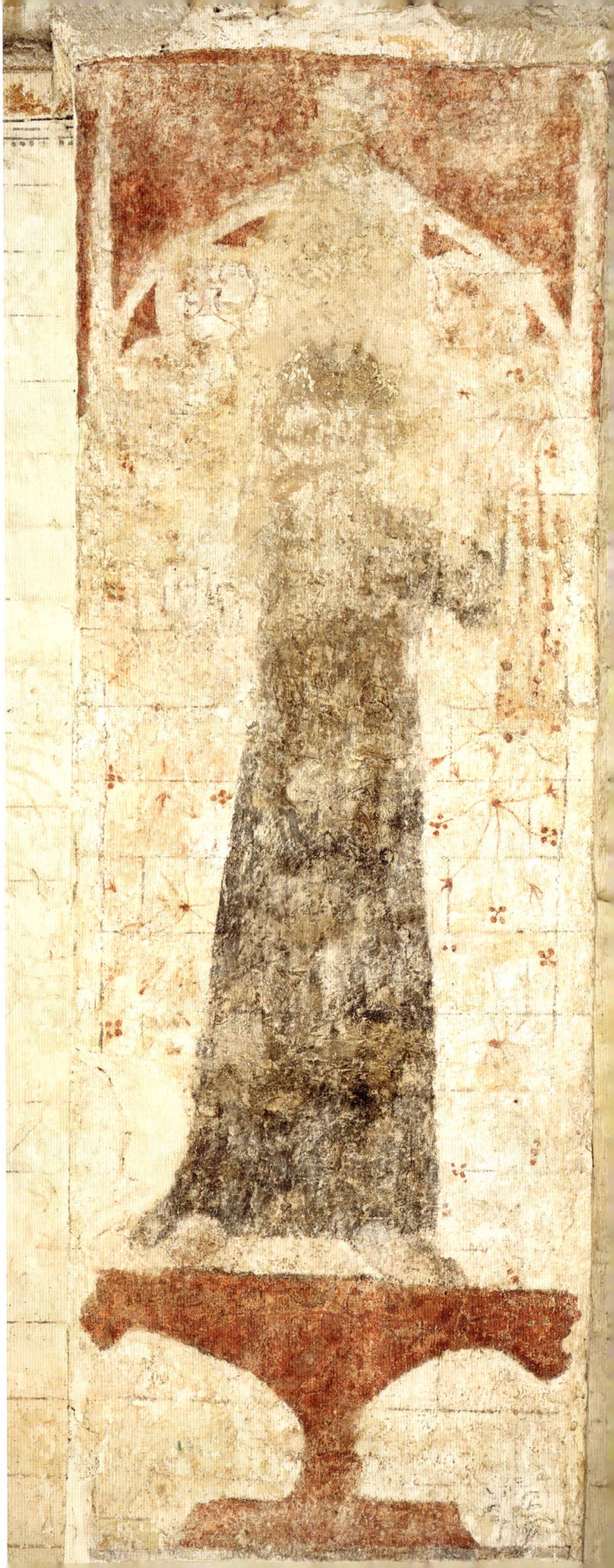

ST SITHA, FROM THE BUONVISI ORPHREYS, STONYHURST COLLEGE, LANCASHIRE

Over 50 images of St Sitha have survived from before the Reformation in England. Her cult in England was well developed long before her body was exhumed in 1560, and she was only canonised in 1696. This embroidery (1490, with repair and additions by Brother Houghton, sacristan of Stonyhurst, *c.* 1827–70) was made for the Buonvisi family, merchants of Lucca, who were based in London from *c.* 1470. The flowers and the majority of the green, black and blue threads, as well as some of the metal threads, were reworked by Brother Houghton after 1827,[61] but St Sitha retains her original attributes of the ubiquitous rosary and keys, symbolising both the authority of women over the household and her apparent ability (like St Anthony) to find lost objects.

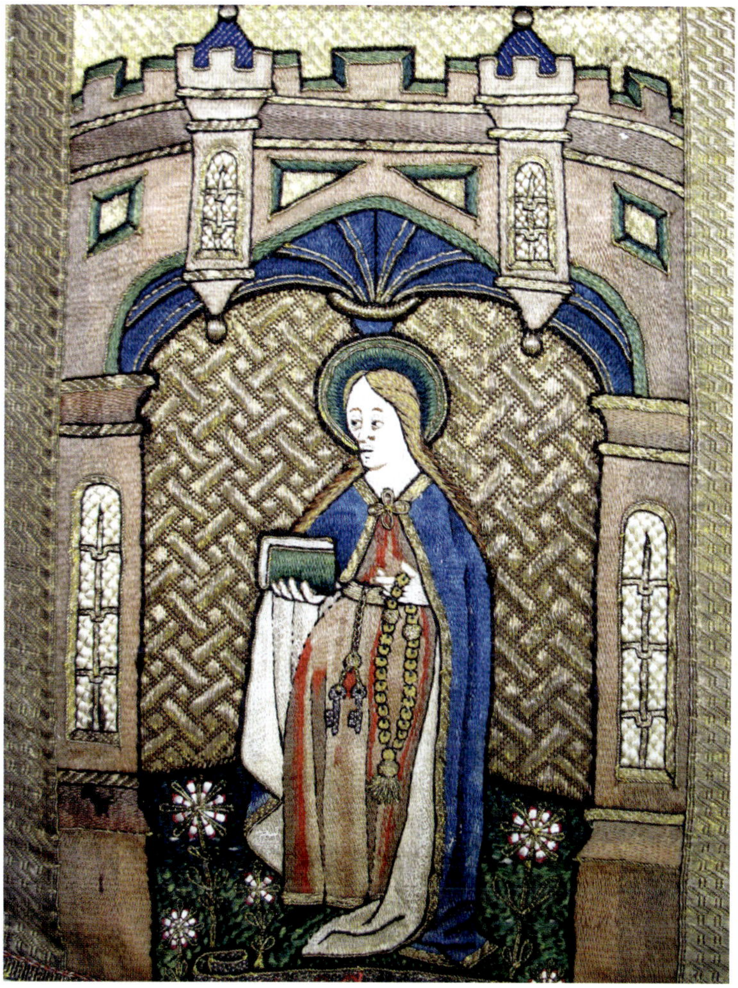

HAIL HOLY SITHA

A prayer in the form of a prose poem attributed to John Lydgate (*c.* 1370–1451) calls on St Sitha to clothe the poor, feed the hungry and, most importantly, restore those things (often keys) lost by 'casual negligence':

Heyl hooly Sitha, maide of gret vertu,
Which with hool herte and devout observaunce
Wer evir besy to serve our lord Iesu,
Nyht and day hym for to do plesaunce,
To poore folk refut of ther grevaunce,
Nakyd to clothe, the hungry for to feede,
Alle disconsolat of feithful attendaunce,
Them to refressh and help them in the[i]r neede.

O Blissid Sitha! flouryng in chastite,
Which of clennesse hast sovereyn excellence
To such as stonde in gret adversite;
For los[s] of good by casuel negligence,
In al such caas do thy dilligence
Them to restoore, to wisse hem, and to Reede,
Geyn worldly trouble and feendys violence,
Supporte alle tho that calle the in the[i]r neede.[62]

STS ALBANS AND AMPHIBALUS

This painting was once thought to represent King Edward the Confessor and St John the Evangelist disguised as a beggar, to whom the saint gave a ring,[63] but it is now clear that St Amphibalus, holding a staff and wearing a pilgrim's scrip (satchel), is giving his cloak and possibly his cross (now missing from the centre of the painting, see p. 47) to St Alban. St Amphibalus's shrine was placed near the rood loft created by Walter of Colchester for Abbot William Trumpington in the nave, at a newly dedicated altar which had a 'superbly painted altarpiece and superaltar'.[64] Traditionally the painting is dated to the early thirteenth century but the slight S-curve of the body and the dress of St Amphibalus, with its hanging sleeves, and the image's similarity to a scene in Matthew Paris's *Life of St Alban* (see p. 47), suggest a date after the middle of the thirteenth century. The earliest lives of Alban recount his conversion by a travelling priest, later called Amphibalus by the chronicler Geoffrey of Monmouth (1095–1155), perhaps in reference to the priest's cloak Alban used as a disguise (from the Latin *'caracalla'*, cloak, into the Greek *amphiballo*).[65] Bede, in his *Ecclesiastical History of the English People*, explains that 'Alban, though still a heathen at the time, gave hospitality to a certain cleric who was fleeing from his persecutors', offered himself to the soldiers wearing the priest's cloak, and was martyred in his place.[66]

The heads of Alban and Amphibalus have not been erased, but the same type of cross-hatched defacement found on the other nave paintings can be seen in the centre above the two figures. Such defacement was reserved for the heads of figures on the south faces of the nave piers and indicates that there was a later painting of a standing figure on top of what we now see, which was scraped away when the images were uncovered in the middle of the nineteenth century. The plinths on which St Sitha and Sts Alban and Amphibalus stand are not used in the first two painted piers and this may indicate that the lost figure stood on a plinth and was contemporary with that of St Sitha. She and the lost figure probably date to the later fourteenth or early fifteenth centuries.

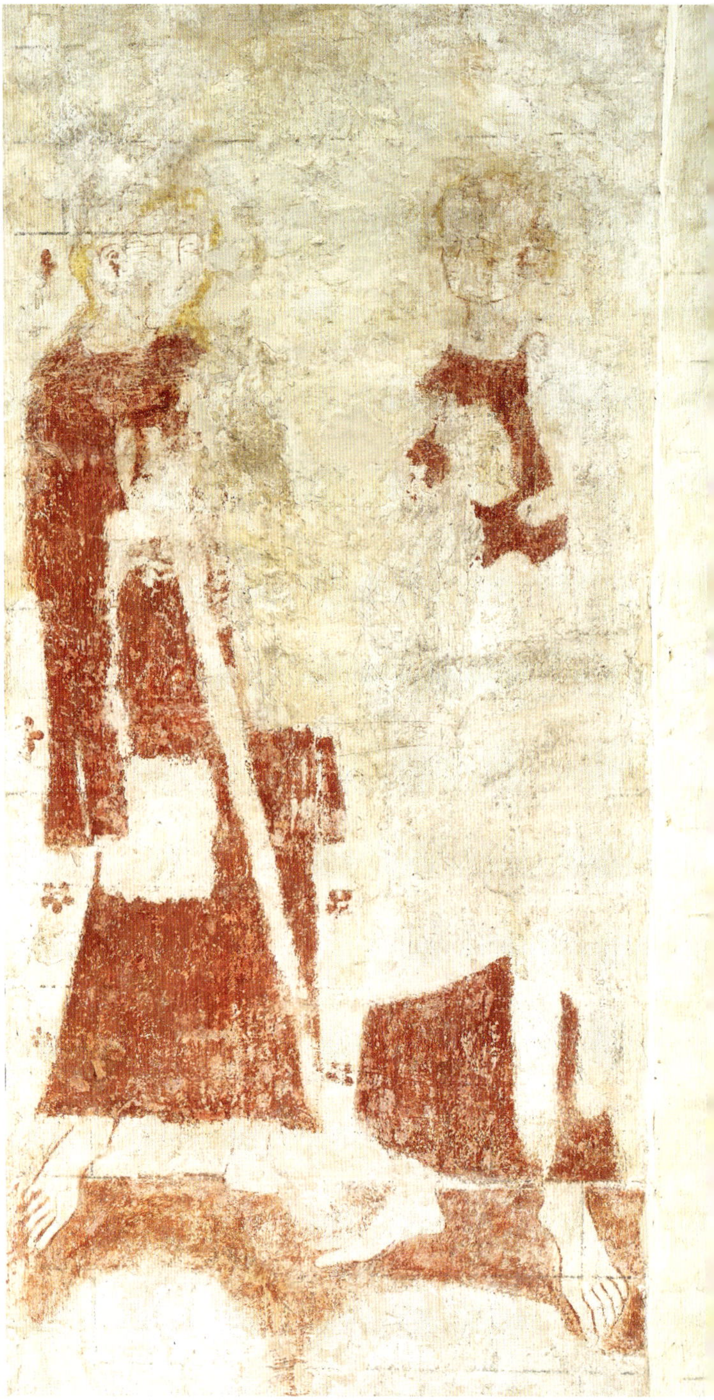

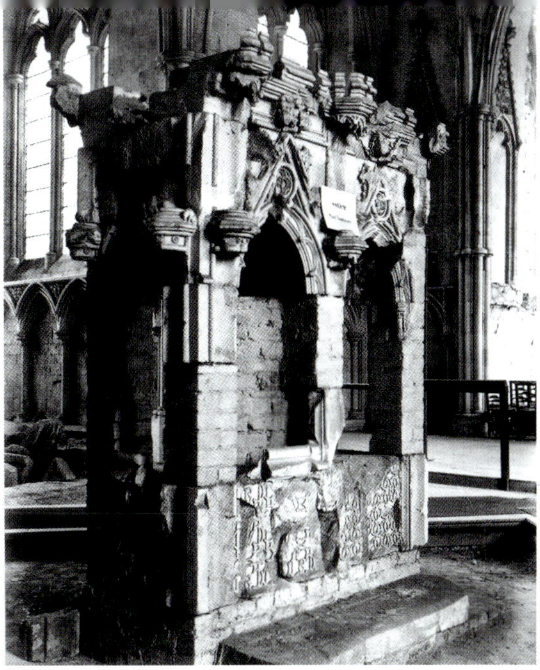

SHRINE OF ST AMPHIBALUS, PHOTOGRAPHED IN 1890

According to the *Chronica Maiora* of Matthew Paris, the relics of St Amphibalus were discovered at Redbourn in 1177 and brought to St Albans.[67] The *Gesta Abbatum* tells us that by 1186 the relics of St Amphibalus and his companions were placed in a reliquary decorated with scenes of his life, near the high altar and the shrine of St Alban in the presbytery. Under Abbot William Trumpington, the reliquary was moved to a place near the rood loft and the altar of the Holy Cross at the east end of the nave, protected by its own iron railings. After the collapse of the south side of the nave in 1323, the rood loft was replaced by the current nave screen *c.* 1350. The reliquary was then moved temporarily to a position immediately behind that of the altar of St Hugh, near the shrine of St Alban at the east end of the church. It finally found a resting place during the abbacy of Thomas de la Mare (1349–96), when the sacrist Ralph Whytechirche, whose initials RW are carved into the fretwork panels of the plinth, paid for a new shrine base to be placed in the vestibule behind the chapel of St Alban.

During the Reformation the bases for both St Alban's and St Amphibalus's shrines were smashed and used as rubble for the walling up of the east end, but parts of these bases were rediscovered in 1872.[68] The Amphibalus shrine base was then reconstructed and placed in the vestibule in front of the Lady Chapel, where it had been erected in the fourteenth century. It was later moved to the north ambulatory.

STS ALBAN AND AMPHIBALUS, FROM MATTHEW PARIS, *LIFE OF ST ALBAN*

During the twelfth century, Brother William of St Albans produced a Latin prose life of St Alban that elaborated on the Anglo-Saxon tradition largely transmitted though Bede.[69] Amphibalus's bones were found soon after at Redbourn, Hertfordshire, as illustrated by Matthew Paris in his *Chronica Maiora*, which shows Robert Mercer, a citizen of St Albans to whom Alban himself had come in a vision, pointing out where Amphibalus was buried.[70] Matthew also translated into Anglo-Norman French and illustrated part of William's account *c.* 1240–50, in a book that took pride of place in *'armariolo A'* (library cupboard A) in the St Albans library (now in Trinity College Dublin). Here Amphibalus hands over his distinctive

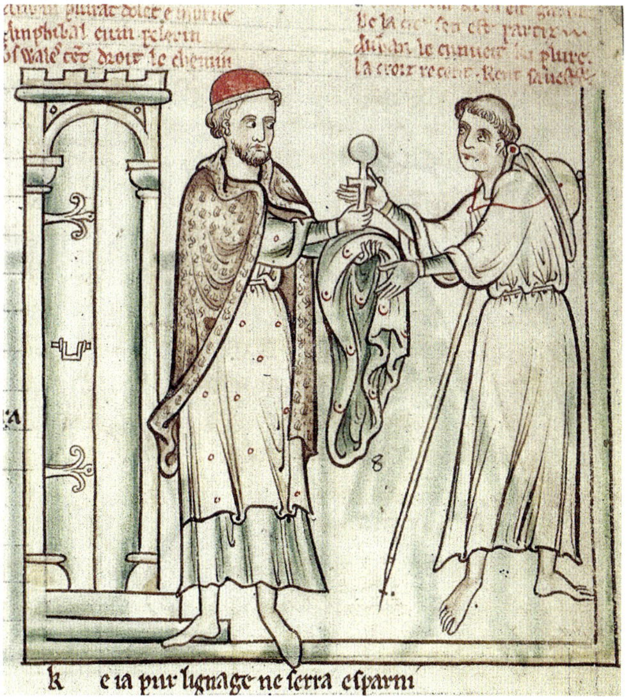

annular or ring-shaped cross to Alban, together with his cloak.[71] Matthew's text refers to Abbot William of Trumpington bringing back this cross 'which had stayed hidden for a long time in London', also noting 'as it is stated in the *History of Sts Alban and Amphibalus*, it was smeared with the blood of St Alban when he was beheaded, and it was the first to be brought into Britain'.[72]

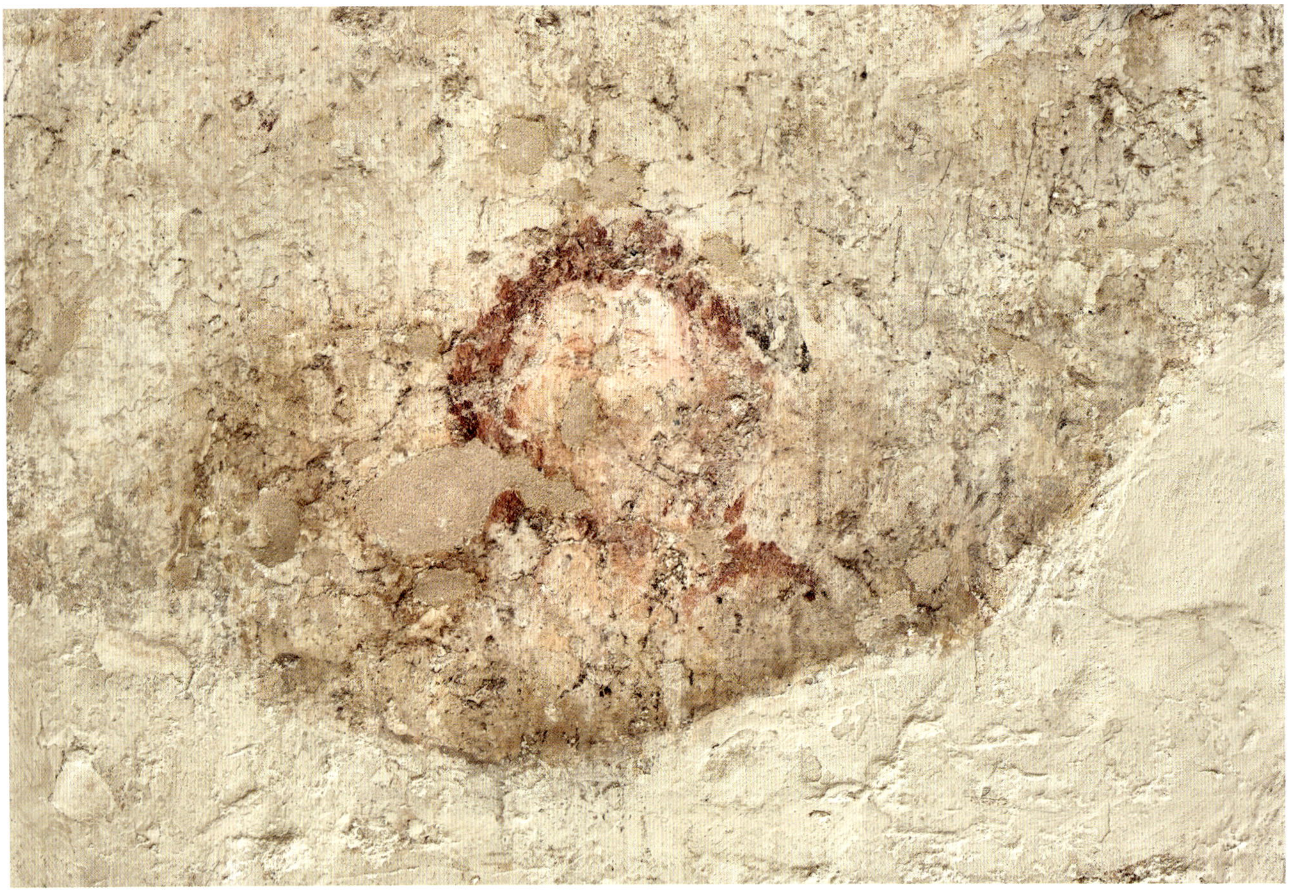

HEAD OF CHRIST(?)

Above the head is a fifteenth-century inscription in Anglo-Norman French which was read by Ridgway Lloyd in the nineteenth century as *'P(riez) pu [r l'almes de] Willelme iadis bal[liuo]: e io[h]anne sa femme e pur l'alme Will[elme]'* (pray for the souls of William formerly bailiff and his wife Johanna and for the soul of William). This may refer to William Tod or Toode (died after 1438), whose wife Johanna died in childbirth in 1430 and who is known to have been bailiff and collector of rents in St Albans in 1429.[73] Amundesham, writing in 1428, states that William Toode and his wife were buried in the north aisle of the nave and that they 'gave to this Church a tenement formerly belonging to Richard Bowyer, alienated for many years from the right of possession by the chapel of the Blessed Virgin. They, led by conscience, restored it, when on their death-bed, to the aforesaid Chapel ...'. The head below the inscription can be dated to the early fourteenth century on stylistic grounds and may belong to a different scheme, while the inscription may well refer to a figure that was once painted over the existing figures of Sts Alban and Amphibalus on the same pier, probably in the fifteenth century (see p. 46).

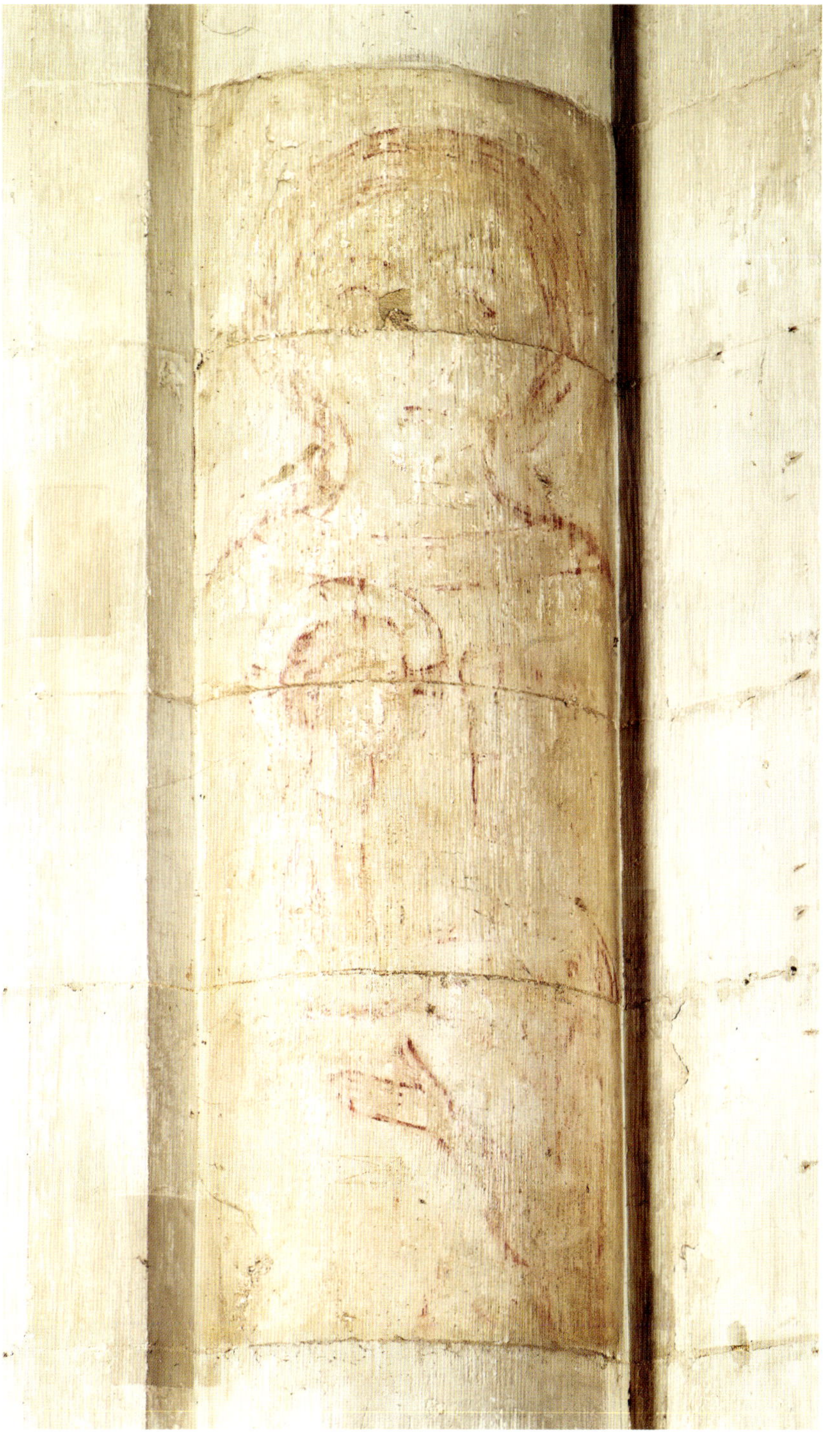

VIRGIN AND CHILD(?)

This image, from the chapel of the Blessed Virgin of the Pillar on the south side of the nave, has been taken to be an Adoration of the Magi, painted across the remodelled Romanesque shafts, but it is more likely to be a representation of the Virgin and Child with the praying hands of William Wyntyrshulle below.[74] The *Annals of St Albans* records that: 'There is an altar before the image of the Blessed Virgin Mary in (the south aisle) erected by the care and at the expense of our brother William Wyntyrshulle; and during all his time very handsomely kept up.' Wyntyrshulle (or Wintershill) was buried in the nave 'opposite the iron gate that closes the Chapel of the Blessed Virgin Mary near to the pillar'. He was 'almoner of this church and chaplain to four Abbots and cross-bearer; a man of great learning ... he furnished the same chapel of St Mary with books and vestments and other requisites for the altar in various ways according to the requirements of the festivals'. At his death, *c.* 1424, he bequeathed a book found in his cell in 'disordered quires' which contained copies of the *Chronica Maiora* with continuations by Thomas of Walsingham, the *Gesta Abbatum* and the *Liber Benefactorum* of St Albans, as well as a chronicle up to the period of Henry IV which he appears to have written himself.[75]

APOSTLES AND PROPHETS(?)

The St Albans 'apostles' are the only surviving examples in England of standing painted figures placed between the clerestory windows of the quire in a major church. This may be because of the unique combination here of Romanesque fabric, with its wide plastered surfaces, and later gothic renovation; the older surfaces acted as a canvas for painted embellishment. Apostles and prophets between clerestory windows feature in early medieval painting schemes such as that at St Georg Oberzell, Reichenau, Germany (1000). Apostles and prophets were also used in programmes of stained glass (Lyons Cathedral *c.* 1235–40) and in sculpture (Cologne Cathedral *c.* 1280). In all these cases the figures act as guardians of a holy space: too high up to have any didactic purpose, their presence served to demarcate the status of the quire in the hierarchy of functions within the church.

Only four figures have survived, three on the north side and one on the south, from what was probably a much bigger scheme. A crenellated parapet can be detected at the feet of the figures on the north side of the quire, which continues into the empty space on either side of the figures, suggesting that each of the 18 available spaces once held figures, and that prophets as well as apostles may have been painted there. In at least two, St John the Evangelist (?) and St James the Greater, the hairstyles are similar to illuminated manuscripts associated with Westminster, such as the *Libellus Geomancie* (book of divination) made for Richard II *c.* 1391–99, and with the ceiling paintings of the Lady Chapel at Abingdon Abbey, Oxon (1391), although the St Albans figures were probably executed slightly earlier.[76]

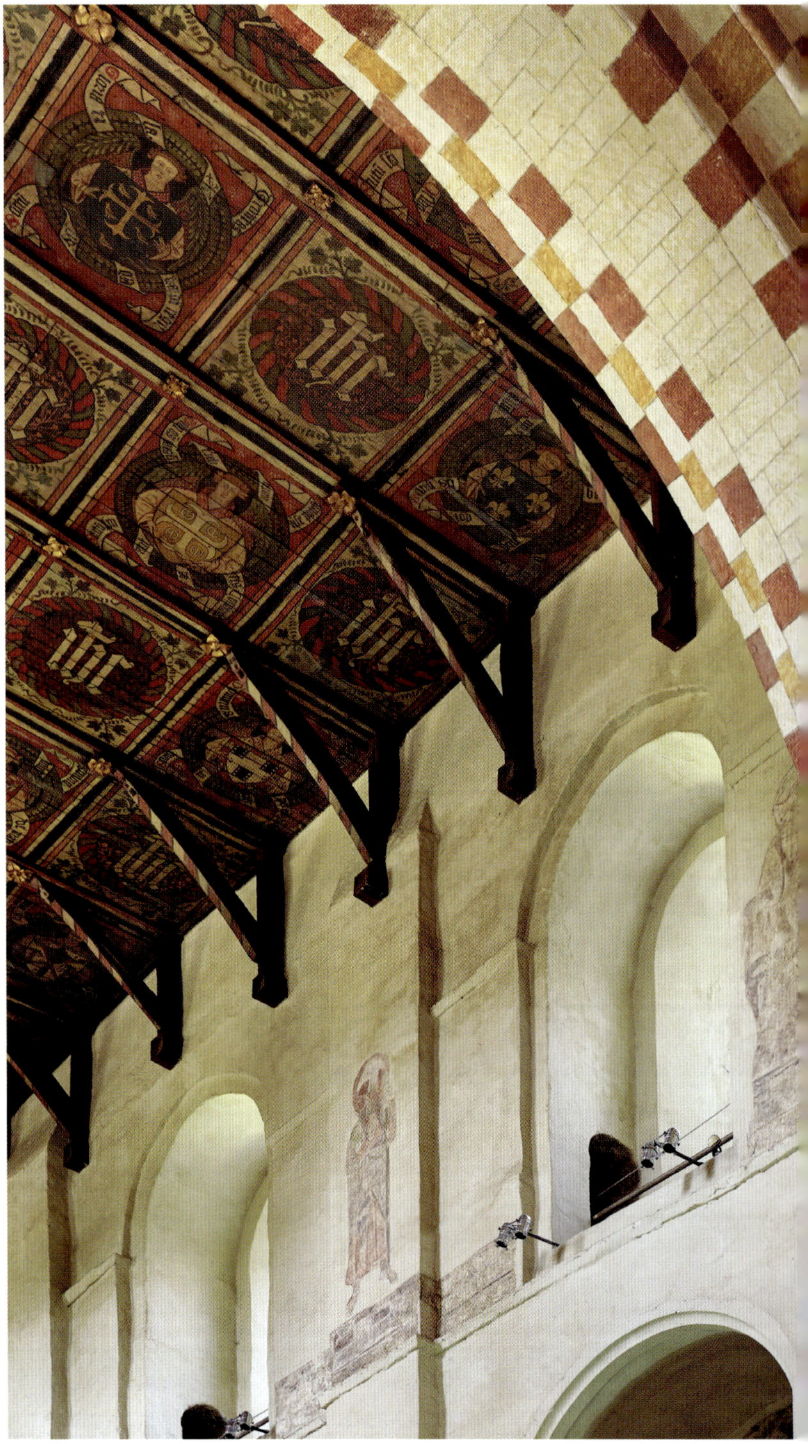

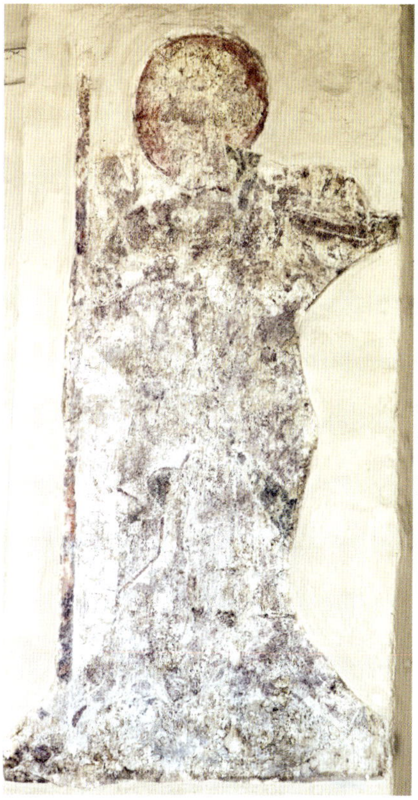

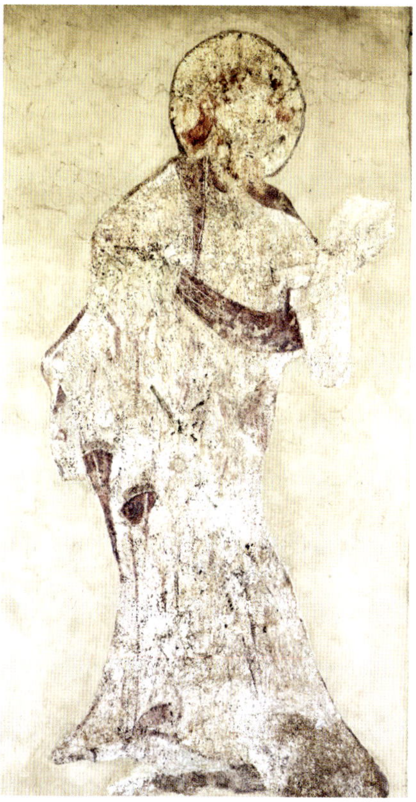

APOSTLE (ST THOMAS?)

(above left)

A long staff or spear is delineated on the left-hand side of this figure; St Thomas Apostle is often shown carrying both a spear and a book, as can be seen on the rood screens at Old Hunstanton, Cawston and Ranworth, all in Norfolk.

APOSTLE (OR PROPHET?)

(above right)

This figure turns to what may be a book in his left hand and he may once have held another attribute in his right hand. Many apostles (especially evangelists) carry books, but he may also represent a prophet. Below his feet, evidence of a crenellated parapet can just be seen.

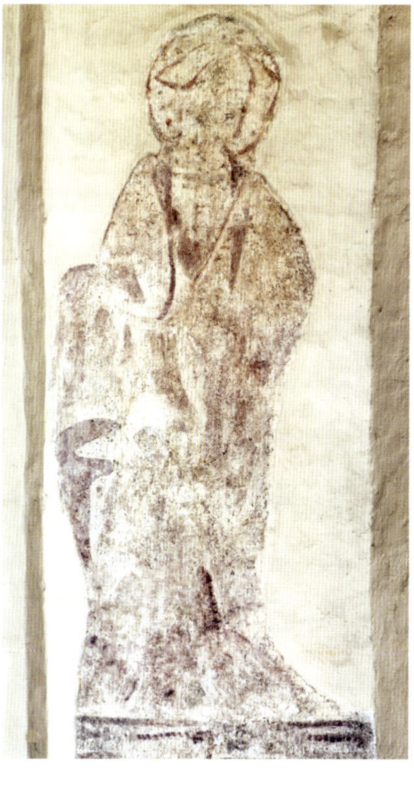

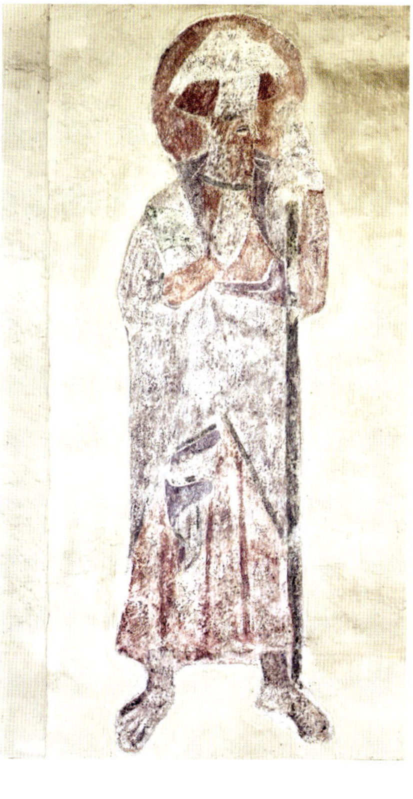

APOSTLE (ST JOHN THE EVANGELIST OR ST BARTHOLOMEW?)

(below left)

He carries a book in his left hand and a small triangular object in his right hand, which has been interpreted as a palm, a popular attribute in England of St John the Evangelist. The shortness of the object could alternatively suggest the knife used in the martyrdom of St Bartholomew, who was flayed alive.

APOSTLE (ST JAMES THE GREATER)

(below right)

The apostle is shown with the pilgrim's travelling hat and staff. The best preserved of the figures, his hair and face suggest a date of *c.* 1375–90, which can be applied to all the surviving figures.

CENSING (?) ANGEL

One of what was originally a pair of angels in the spandrels on either side of the south ambulatory arch, this figure is usually dated to the early thirteenth century. It has been associated with a statue of the Virgin, which we learn from Matthew Paris was called the 'Mariola' and was carved by Walter of Colchester during the abbacy of William of Trumpington. An oblique reference to the renovation of the ceiling of the south transept, and the whitewashing of the walls of the abbey at the same time, suggests that it stood in the south transept. The placing of such statues on corners, junctions or piers is relatively common and the statue may have been in closer proximity to the angel than might appear. Although the angel's face appears to be in keeping with a thirteenth-century date, however, the intrados (underside) of the outer arch is decorated with a three-dimensional scroll running around an inner bar, which is characteristic of decorative schemes of the early fifteenth century. The wings of the angel, on which a considerable amount of green paint survives, may also have been repainted at a later date.

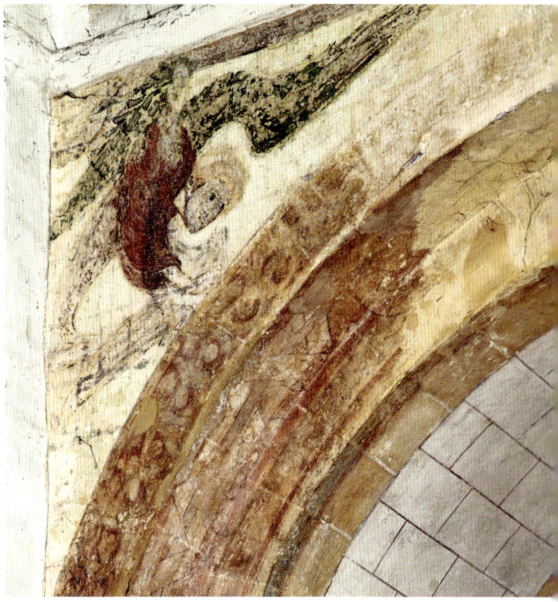

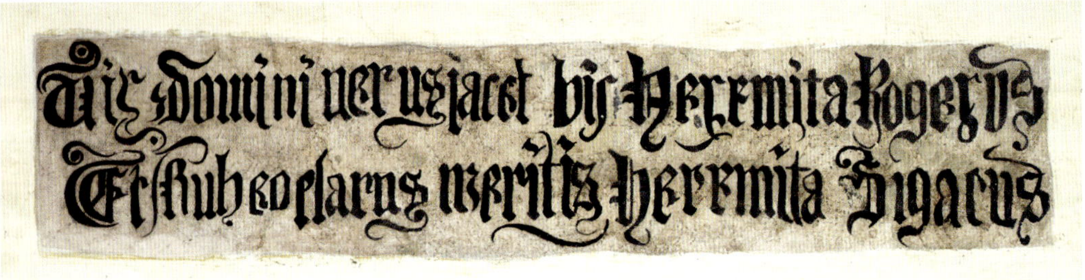

TOMB OF SIGAR OF NORTHAW AND ROGER OF MARKYATE

This inscription on the south wall of the nave aisle reads *'Vir domini verus jacet hic hermita Rogerus / Et sub eo clarus meritis hermita Sigarus'* (a true man of God, the hermit Roger lies here /and beneath him the famous hermit Sigar). In his description of the altars and monuments at St Albans, written *c.* 1428, John Amundesham states: 'There is also nigh unto the door of the Church leading to the cloister, in an arch recess of the wall, the tomb of Roger, a Hermit and deacon, a man remarkable for sanctity; beneath him lies Sigar the hermit, his fellow in holiness and in merits. Their miraculous life is to be seen inscribed upon a tablet over their graves.' The current inscription, which may date to *c.* 1500, probably records part of this lost tablet.

Roger was a monk of St Albans who lived as a hermit in a cell at Markyate, Hertfordshire. For four years the anchoress and later prioress Christina of Markyate (1096–1155) also lived there, in a tiny cell 'near the chapel of the old man ... it had a plank of wood set before it, and it was so concealed that to anyone looking from outside it would seem that no one could possibly be inside, since the place was no bigger than a span and a half' (about 36 cms).[77] Sigar, who had a cell at Northaw, Herts, attended services at St Albans by walking to the abbey each day; the *Gesta Abbatum* records that his prayers expelled the nightingales from around his cell as they were disturbing him.

DOUBTING OF ST THOMAS

This painting, the survivor of two scenes described by John Amundesham in the fifteenth century (see Tomb of Sigar, p. 52) as showing the 'History of the Passion' and the 'History of the Resurrection', stands apart from most English medieval wall paintings because of the ambition of its architectural construction. Only in the (now lost) paintings on the east wall of St Stephen's chapel at Westminster (*c.* 1355–63?) has evidence survived of an earlier attempt at such a complex *trompe l'oeil* architectural arrangement. One of the best-preserved of the wall paintings in the abbey, the Doubting of St Thomas – showing Christ after the Resurrection – still displays rich reds and greens, while the faces of Christ and St Thomas are unmarked by defacement. The scene is placed on a tiled floor, under a complex perspectival vaulted structure seen from below. Remarkably, this unusual architectural ensemble can also be found framing the Annunciation miniature in *Les Petites Heures*, an illuminated book of hours made for Jean, duc de Berry *c.* 1384–90 under the supervision of Jacquemart de Hesdin.[78] The Doubting of St Thomas is usually dated to the early fifteenth century and was certainly painted before 1428, when Amundesham was writing. The confident handling of the architecture also recalls work in the Carmelite Missal associated with artists who may have migrated to England from the Netherlands, suggesting a date for the wall painting of between 1390 to1410.[79]

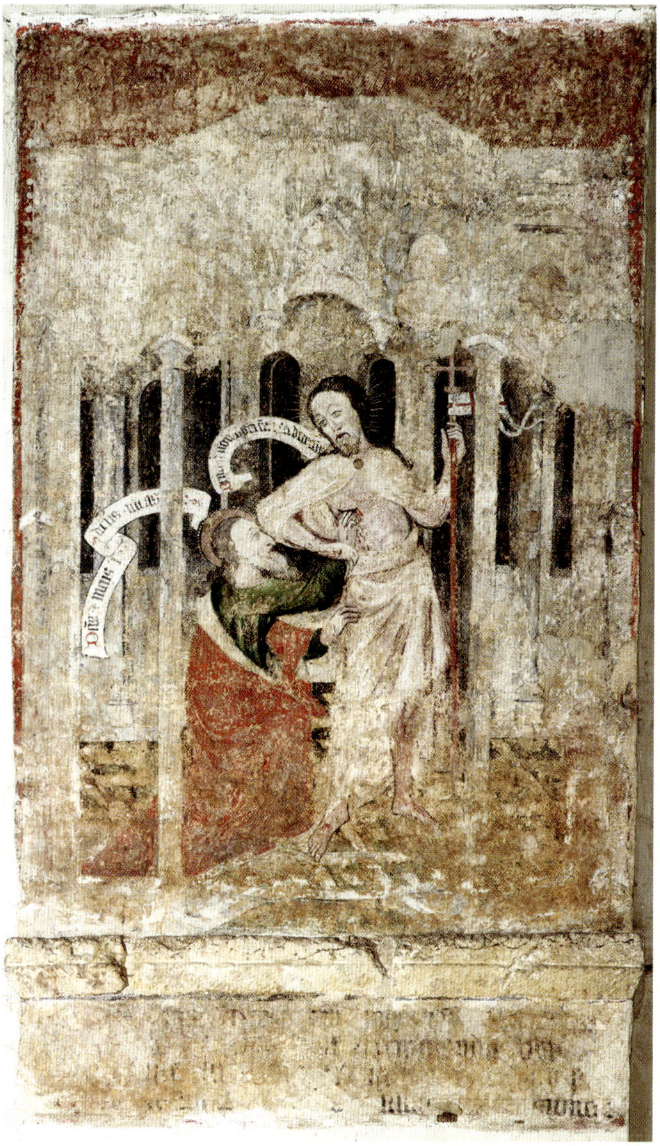

The speech scroll that emerges from behind St Thomas reads *'Dominus meus et Deus meus'* (my Lord and my God), while that for Christ reads '*Beati qui non viderunt, et credierunt*' (blessed are they that have not seen and yet have believed), taken from St John's Gospel (20: 29). Amundesham records the now only partially surviving inscription below, which linked the two scenes: *'Mors tua, mors Christi, fraus mundi, gloria coeli / Et dolor inferni, sint memoranda tibi / In cruce sum pro te; qui peccas desine, pro me / Desine condono; pugna, juvo; vince, corono'* (your death, Christ's death, deceitful world, heaven's glory / and the pains of hell are a reminder / I was on the cross for you; you who sin, stop, for me / cease [and] I pardon; fight [and] I help; conquer [and] I crown).

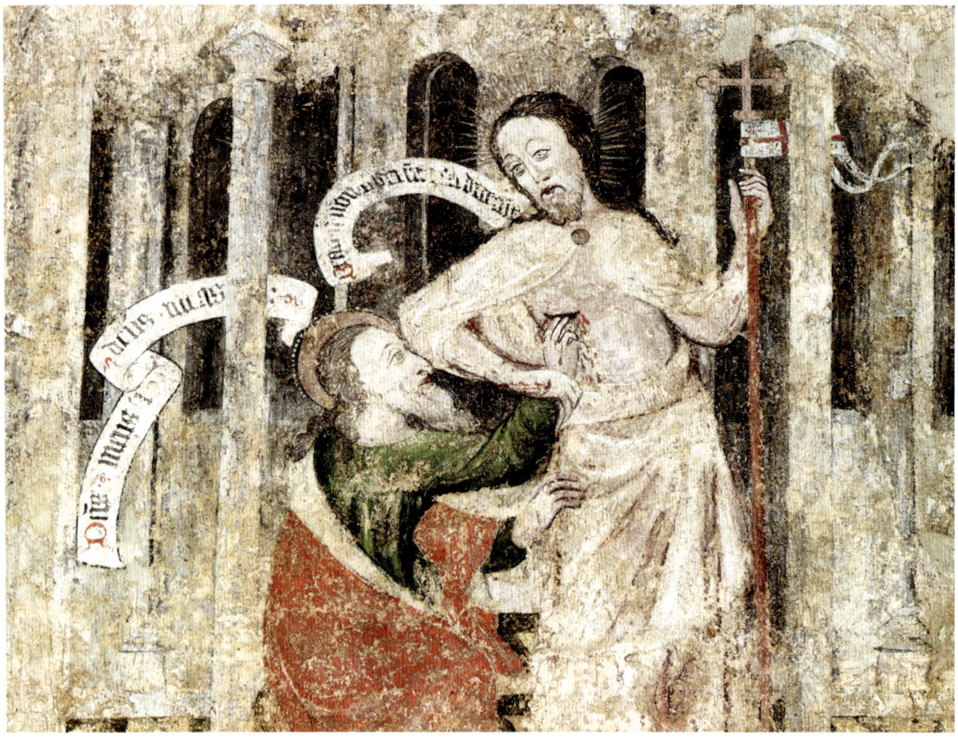

DOUBTING OF ST THOMAS

(left, detail)

Christ holds the *vexillum* (flag of victory over death) in his left hand and takes St Thomas's wrist in his left hand, thrusting it into the wound in his side. The kneeling St Thomas stares intently at the wound. Christ's naked chest is revealed beneath his white cloak, which is fastened by a small circular golden morse (clasp).

DOUBTING OF ST THOMAS, WESTMINSTER ABBEY *(right)*

This painting, which forms a pair with the St Christopher in the next bay of the south transept arcade at Westminster Abbey (see p. 41, above), is one of a group that has been associated with Walter of Durham (active *c.* 1265–1304). He was employed as a 'King's Painter' by Henry III, while Edward I commissioned him in 1296 to produce the painted and gilded coronation chair to house the stone of Scone. The awkwardness of Christ's gesture in grabbing Thomas's wrist does not follow the traditional iconography of the *ostentatio vulnerum* (display of the wound), common since early Christian times, where Christ raises his right arm to let Thomas place his fingers in the wound. The wrist-holding gesture should rather be associated with the innovative iconographies demanded by Henry III, who was also the first in England to introduce images of St Christopher, which he had painted in his and the queen's chapels.

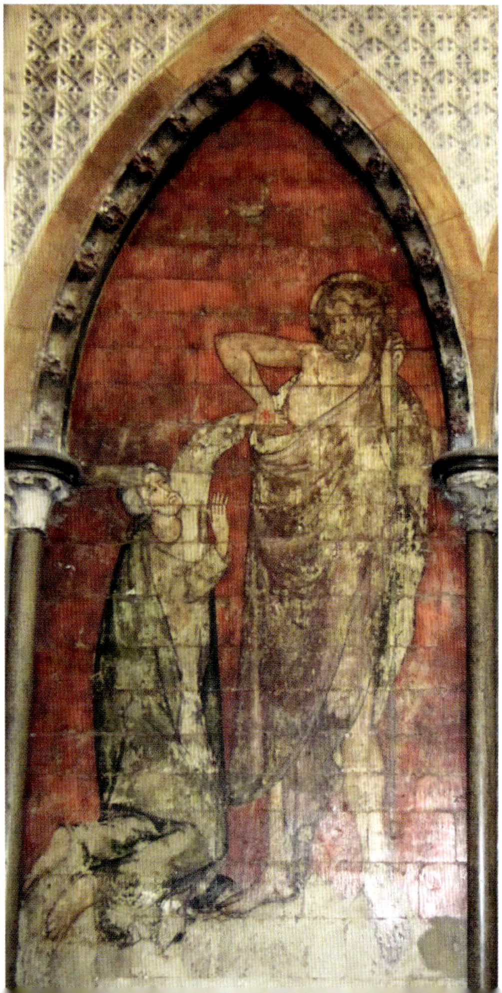

DOUBTING OF ST THOMAS

(opposite, detail)

St Thomas gazes directly at Christ's wound, reflecting the words on the scroll that those who have not seen, and yet believe, are blessed, which are taken from the antiphon for vespers on the octave of Easter Sunday. The display of the wound also holds a eucharistic meaning, recalling the ceremony of the Last Supper at which consecrated bread and wine are consumed in commemoration of Christ's sacrifice.

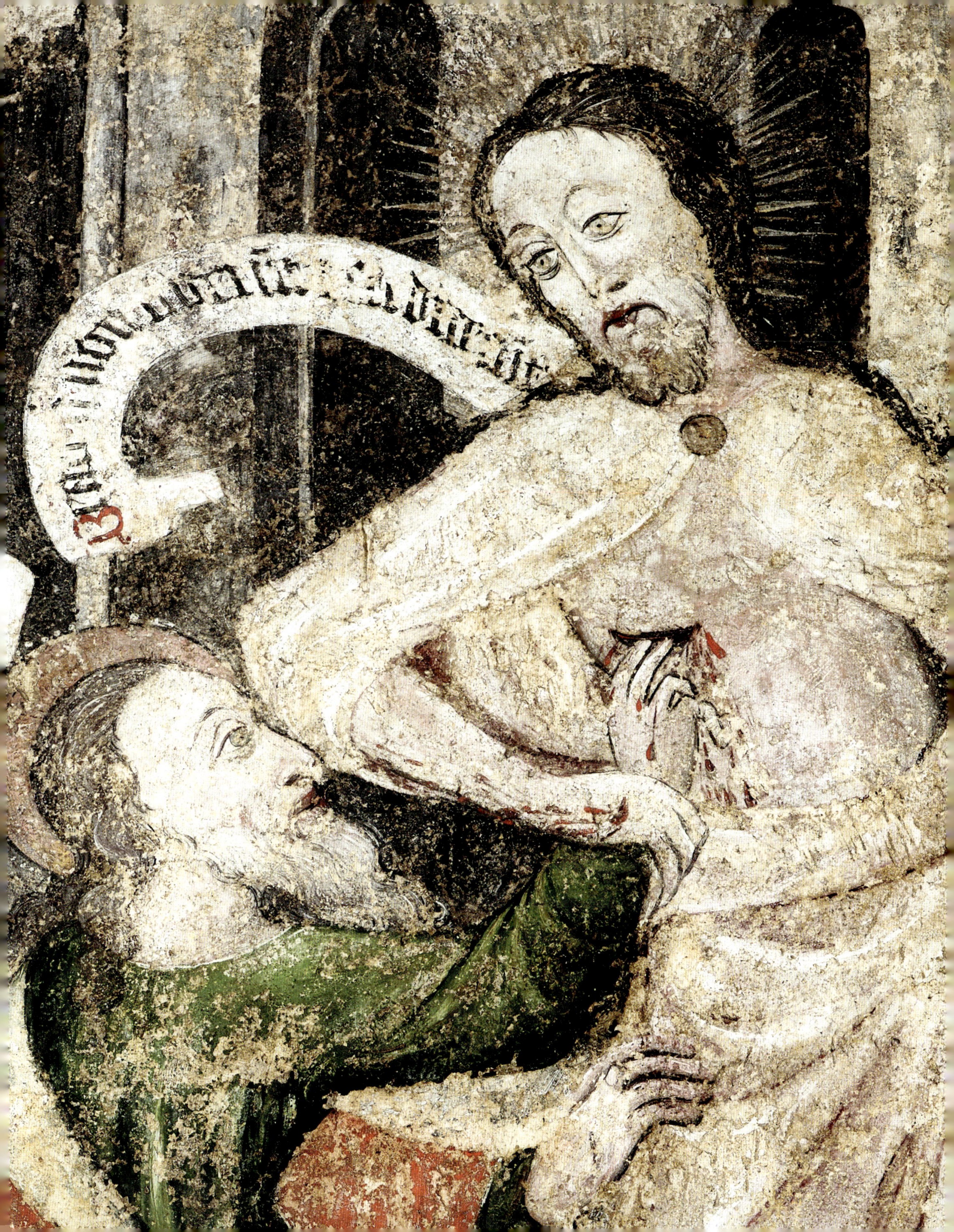

ARMORIALS

The late fifteenth-century ceiling of the tower was frequently repainted but now lies underneath a modern reconstruction of the original, based on the investigations of Clive Rouse in 1951.[80] The armorials that were uncovered and reproduced are those of *France quartering England* (for the English crown after *c.* 1405); *Azure, a cross patonce between 5 martlets or* (for St Edward the Confessor); *Argent, a cross gules* (for St George) and *Azure, a saltire or* (for St Alban). The ceiling also displays red and white roses, which may be associated with the union of the houses of Lancaster (red) and York (white), after the victory of the future Henry VII over Richard III in 1485 and his marriage to Elizabeth of York in 1486.

Below the ceiling, on the plastered walls of the lantern of the eleventh-century tower, are four large shields, one on each face. These are painted to give the illusion of being hung on leather straps from the walls and were restored by Clive Rouse in 1951. Sculpted shields of the most important members of the royal family and the most powerful families in the England were placed by Henry III in the nave of Westminster Abbey. The painted shields at St Albans, however, relate to Edward I and his immediate family. The shields of England, France, St Edward the Confessor and either St Oswin or St Edmund were also sculpted after 1323 on the rebuilt south nave wall. The absence of Edward III's wife's shield in the nave of St Albans suggests that this display is either meant to represent Edward II (1307–27) and Isabella of France or Edward III and his mother before the end of his minority in 1330, and that they were executed before Abbot Michael of Mentmore (1335–49) completed the ongoing works.

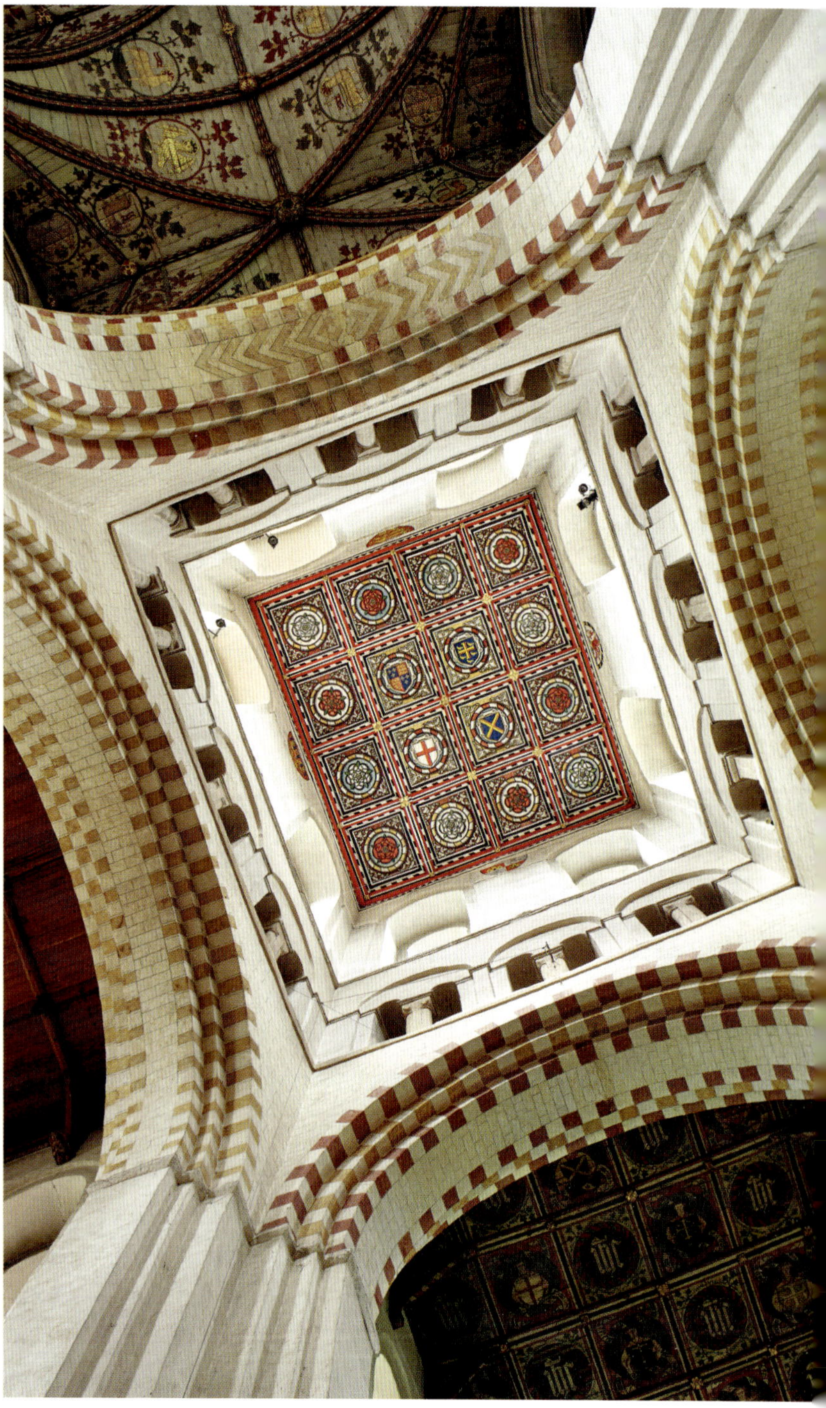

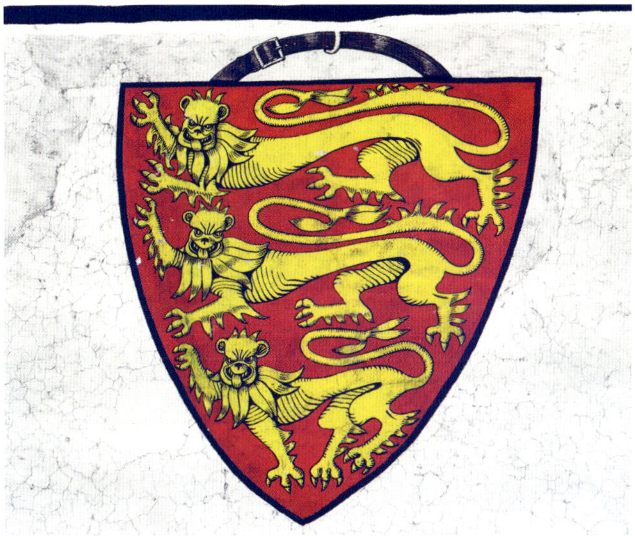

ENGLAND (*left*)

Gules three lions passant guardant or (the lions when shown in this way are also called leopards), arms borne by the English kings from the time of Richard I's second great seal of 1198 until *c.* 1340, when Edward III quartered them with the *fleurs-de-lys* of France.

CASTILE AND LEON (*below*)

Quarterly 1 and 4, *gules a castle or*, 2 and 3, *argent a lion rampant sable*, arms used by Eleanor of Castile, who married Edward I in 1254 at the monastery of Las Huelgas, Burgos, Spain.

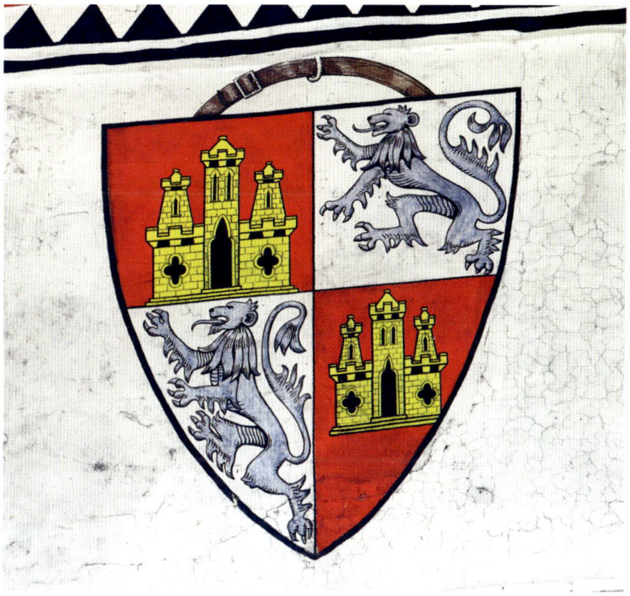

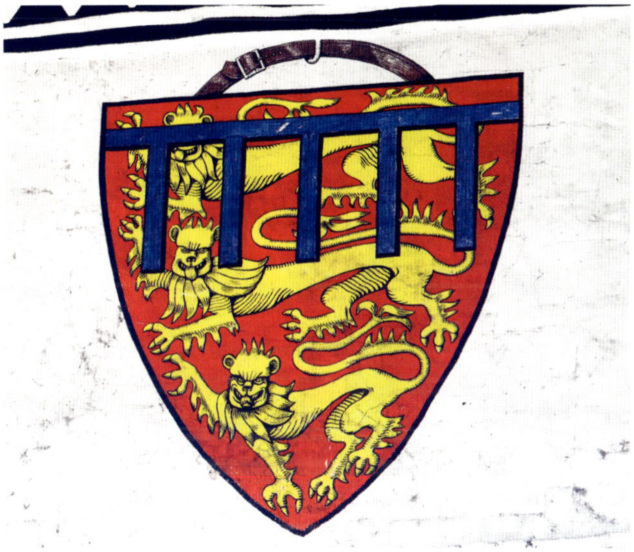

THE KING'S ELDEST SON

(above)

Gules three lions passant guardant or with a label of five points azure, first borne by Prince Alphonso (1273–84) and then by the future Edward II. After 1301 these arms were then borne by the heir to the throne as prince of Wales.

RICHARD OR EDMUND, EARL OF CORNWALL

(right)

Argent, a lion rampant gules crowned or, a bordure sable bezanty, borne by the earls of Cornwall, father Richard (1209–72) and son Edmund (1249–1300). Richard was also count of Poitou; he was elected king of Germany and crowned as king of the Romans at Aachen in 1257.

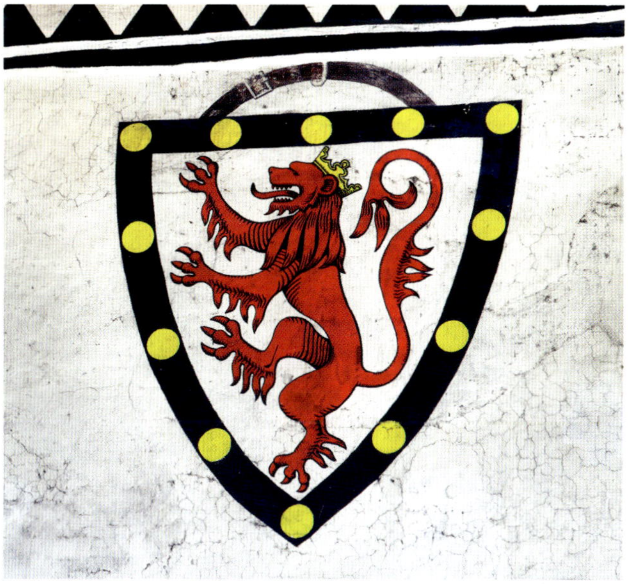

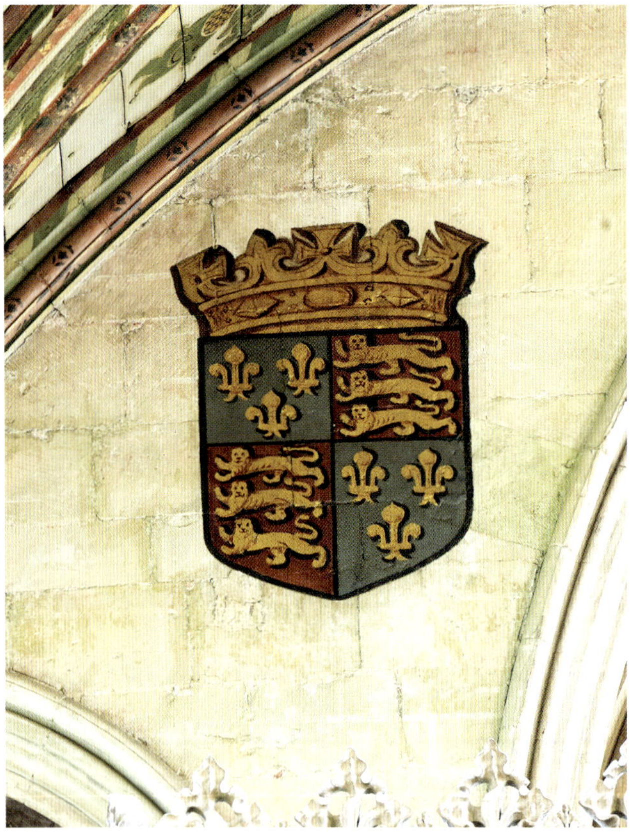

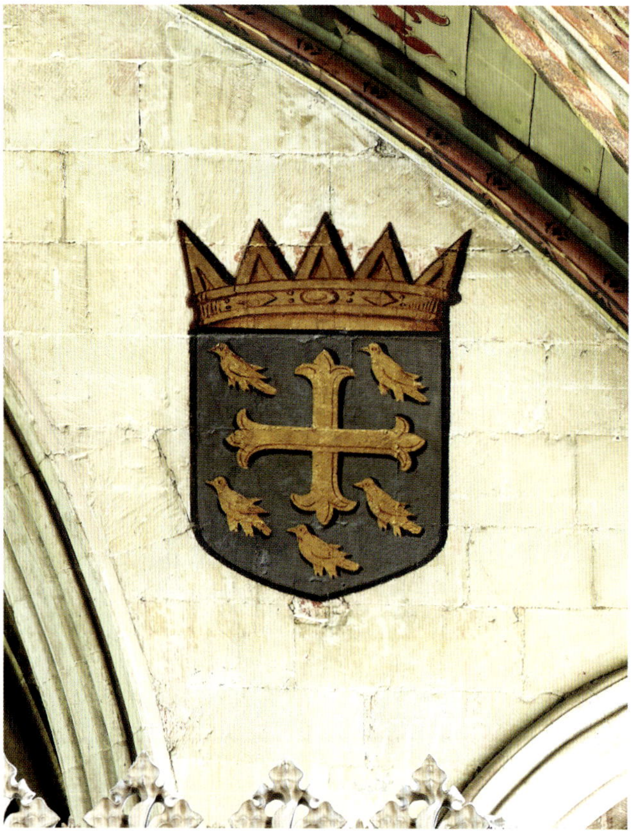

PRESBYTERY EAST WALL, ST ALBAN'S CHAPEL

The far wall of the presbytery, enclosing St Alban's chapel, is now largely obscured by the great screen built by Abbot William Wallingford (1476–92) after 1476. On it are displayed the arms of England as used probably by Henry VII (left), and those of St Edward the Confessor (right).

PRESBYTERY CEILING

Matthew Paris tells us that cracks appeared in the presbytery walls in 1257, making the remodelling of the east end an urgent priority. The wooden vault over the presbytery, put in place by around 1285 after a failed attempt to vault the area in stone, represents a rare survival of English medieval carpentry and is a masterpiece in itself. During cleaning and consolidation of the vault, undertaken firstly by Professor Ernest Tristram *c.* 1931 and more recently in 1997–2002, traces of the original decoration were discovered – a simple foliate scheme that would have been as appropriate to a stone as to a wooden vault. The present scheme was largely undertaken during the abbacy of John of Wheathampstead. It depicts the symbols of St John the Baptist (the lamb and flag) and St John the Evangelist (the eagle), set in roundels from which foliate scrolls emerge, which Abbot John took as his badges.[81]

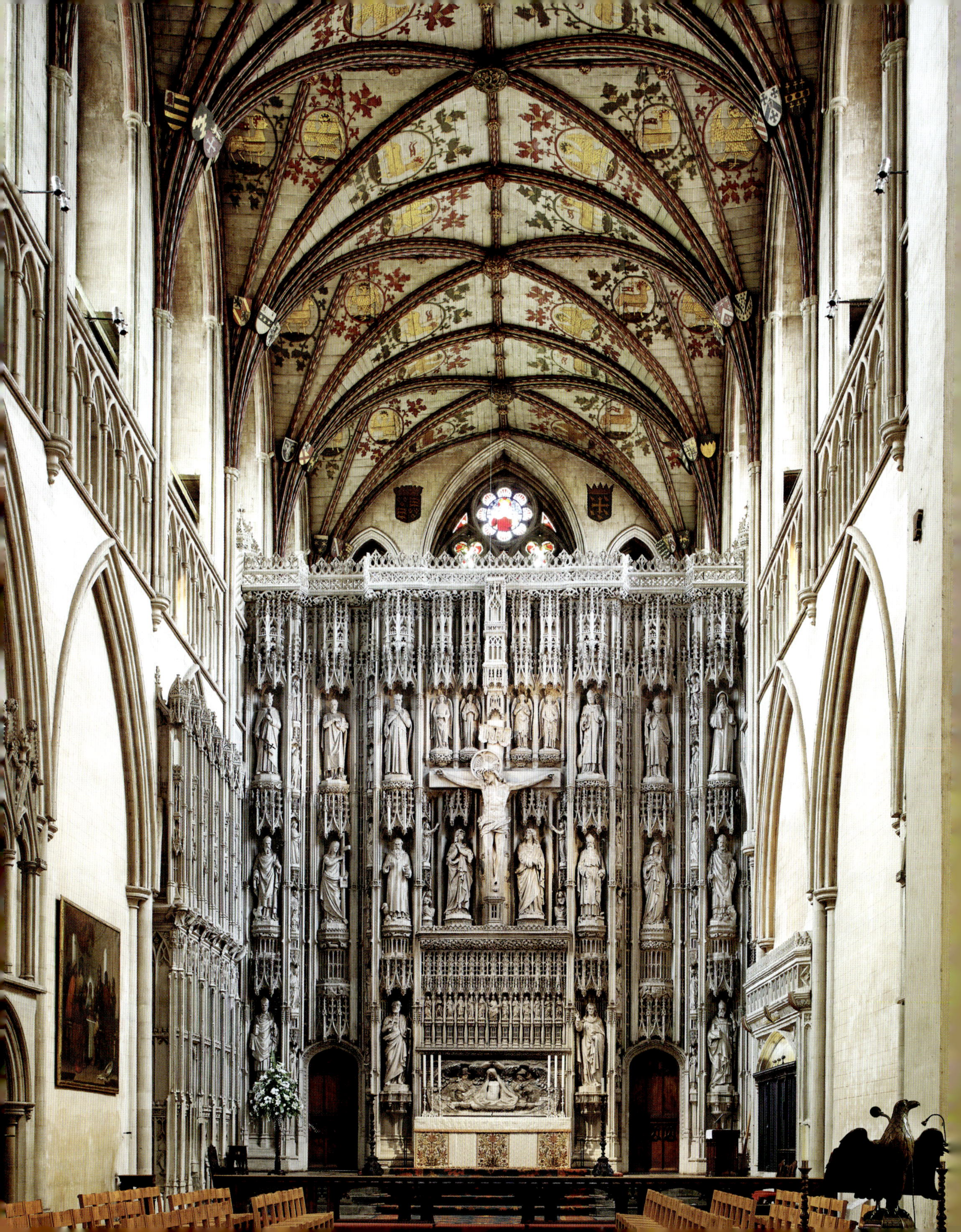

ARMORIALS OF STS OSWIN, ALBAN AND AMPHIBALUS

By including his badges in the vault of the presbytery, Abbot John of Wheathampstead placed his patronage at the heart of the most important part of the building, in full sight of the community at St Albans, if not of God himself. The display of armorials on the west wall of the presbytery reinforces this message. His two badges of the eagle and the lamb are placed between the arms of St Oswin, St Alban and St Amphibalus, while the words *Domine* (Lord) *Miserere* (have mercy) are painted at a 30-degree angle to each other, allowing the now very faint Head of Christ, which belongs to a Majesty scene from a previous scheme of decoration (see p. 62), to remain visible. Below the shields an inscription clarifies his intention: *Sic ubicunque vides sit pictus ut agnus et ales / Effigies operis sexti patris ista Johannis / Esse vel in toto juvis vel in faciendo / Est opus hoc unum causavit eum faciendu[m]* (wherever thou seest thus, that a lamb and a bird are painted, that is the representation of the work of the sixth father John, showing that either he was involved in the whole or he assisted in the making. This work alone was the reason for him to come into being).[82] This clearly refers to all the works that he funded, as the sixth abbot to be called John.

The arms of King Oswin (*gules, three crowns or*) are found in a number of contexts at St Albans, as his relics were held by Tynemouth Priory, a cell of St Albans in Northumbria. Like those of Alban in the centre (*azure a saltire or*) and Amphibalus (*quarterly gules and or, four lions counter-coloured*), they are entirely fictitious. The assumption that both Alban and Amphibalus were of noble birth, and therefore must have borne arms, is implied in the tract *On the Nobility, Lives and Martyrdom of Alban and Amphibalus* which appears to have been written by the monk Thomas of Walsingham when he wrote his continuation of the *Gesta Abbatum*.[83] In this he elaborates on the fictitious stories of Alban and Amphibalus's lives written in the twelfth and thirteenth centuries, and his version is then translated and further embroidered by John Lydgate, at the behest of Abbot John of Wheathampstead. Amphibalus becomes the son of a prince of Wales, and Alban a knight in the service of the emperor Diocletian who is eventually made Steward of Britain: 'Bi comyssion and title Imperiall / Prynce and stiward thoruhout al Briteyn / Albon was chose…'. Thus Lydgate creates a feudal model of knighthood that would be believable in the contemporary context of later medieval England.[84]

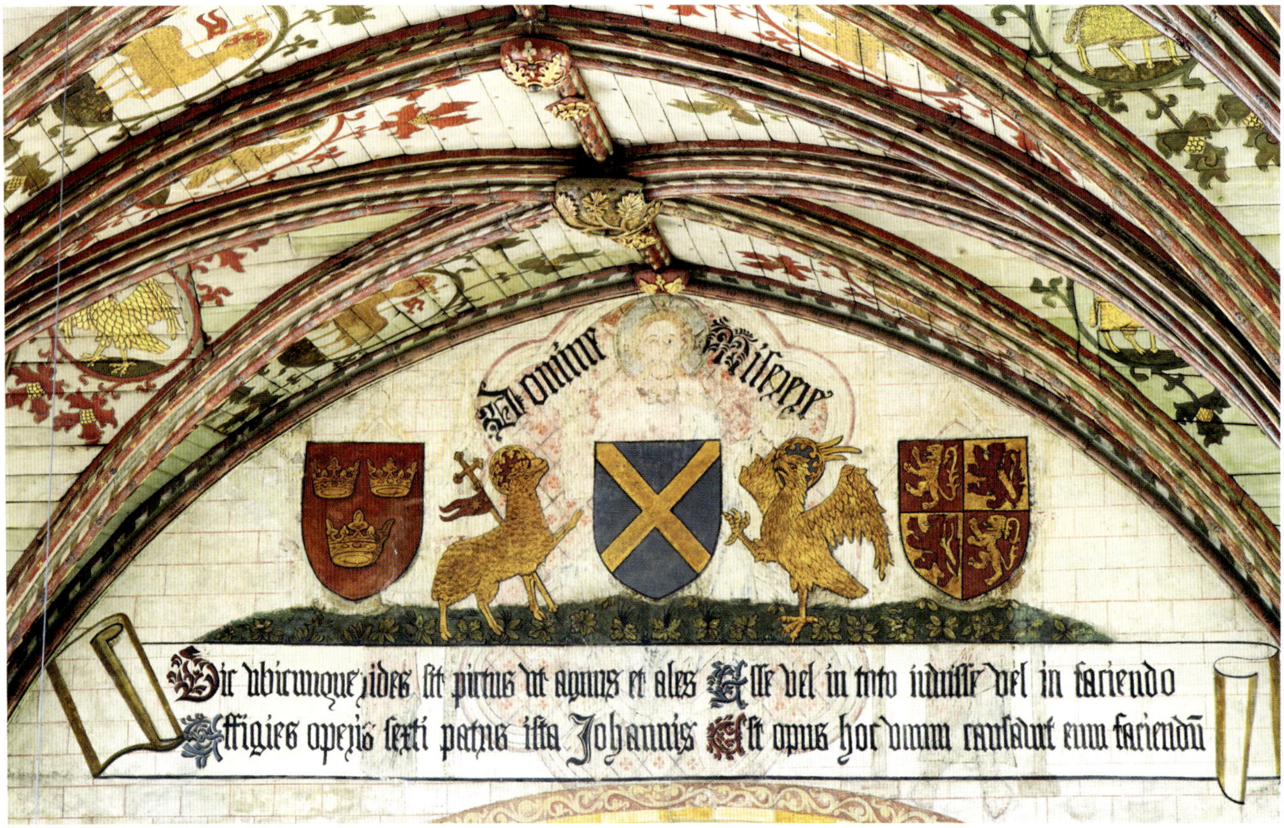

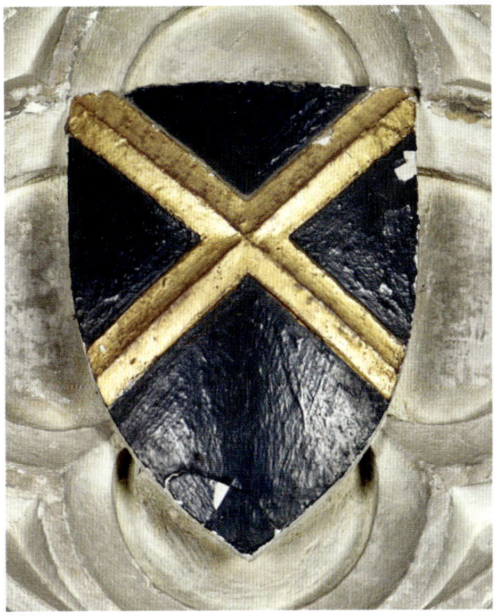

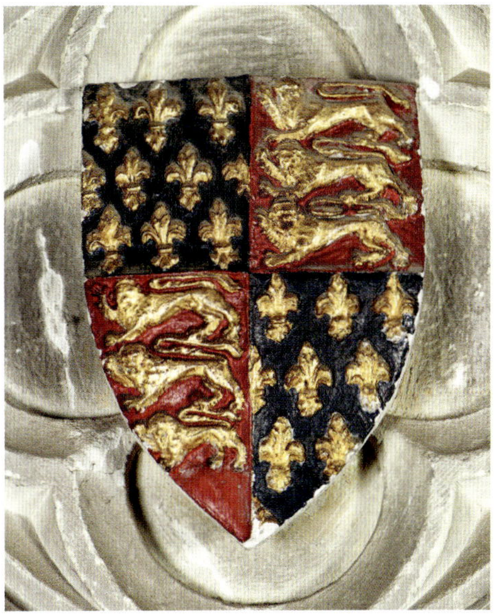

ARMORIAL OF ST ALBAN

The earliest depiction of the armorial of St Alban (*azure, a saltire or*), appears in a French copy of Pope Gregory IX's *Decretals* that also had images added in England *c.* 1330. These armorials were also associated in the fifteenth century with the legendary kings of Mercia, such as King Warremundus of Warwick, as well as with St Alban.[85] By the late fourteenth century they were certainly identified with St Alban, as they feature on a doorway built then, leading from the south aisle of the nave to the cloister (above left), where they are paired with those of *France quartering England*, adopted by Edward III after *c.* 1340 and also used by Richard II (above right). John Beaver, monk of St Albans and prior of Belvoir (a cell of St Albans), who is commemorated by a brass of *c.* 1460–70 now in the presbytery[86] presented a beautifully written and illuminated *Liber de exemplis sacre scripture* (commentaries on the Old Testament) to the abbey library after 1432 and included the arms of Alban in the opening initial (folio 2r) (right).[87] The motto '*Beaver / ab adversis / Albon tueatur / in armis*' (Beaver, in the arms of Alban, be protected from adversity) is written on a scroll surrounding the initial. This suggests that the use of armorials by Wheathampstead on the west wall of the presbytery should be regarded as more than just a whimsical and scholarly allusion; in both cases the shields embodied deeply held beliefs in their apotropaic function to protect the abbey itself.

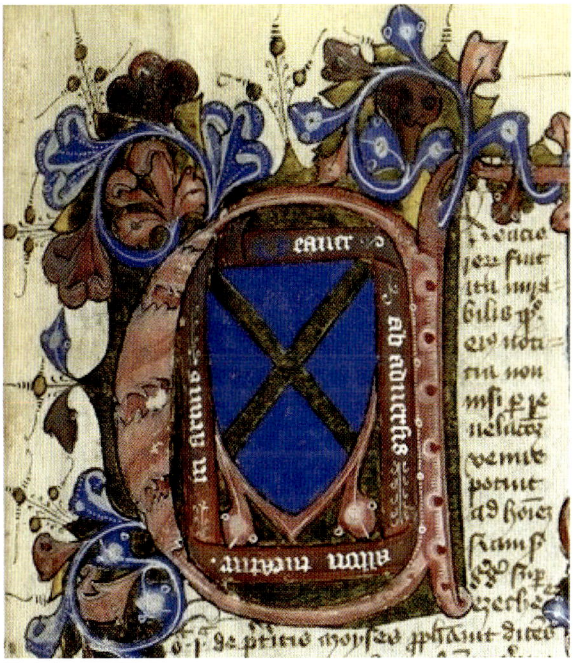

CHRIST IN MAJESTY

When Professor Ernest Tristram was investigating and restoring the paintings on the vault of the presbytery, he discovered the remains of an earlier painting on the west wall, below the shields and inscriptions added by Abbot John of Wheathampstead. As part of his investigations, he always made a watercolour drawing of each of the paintings he studied. In this reconstruction of the three figures he found, held in the cathedral archive, he places keys in the hand of the left-hand figure, the remnants of which are just visible as a diagonal line in the original painting, suggesting that the figure represents St Peter, holder of the keys to heaven. The right-hand figure is then likely to represent St Paul, as they are often found together in early Christian symbolism denoting the *Traditio legis*, the transmission of the law to Peter and Paul by Christ. The central figure, identified by his cross nimbus, blessing hand and the arc of a rainbow on which he sits, is Christ in Majesty. A chalice, still clearly visible in his left hand, suggests a specifically eucharistic message for this iconography. The remains of the architectural canopies framing the two saints also survive, formed by a crocketed gable with pinnacles on either side. They resemble so closely those of the retable made for the high altar of Westminster Abbey, *c.* 1269–72, that it has been suggested that the artist of the painting was familiar with this work of art. There can be no doubting the quality of the St Albans painting, and this may also account for the unusual inclusion of Sts Peter and Paul in the otherwise eucharistic Christ in Majesty iconography, as they also occur in a different context on the Westminster retable.[88]

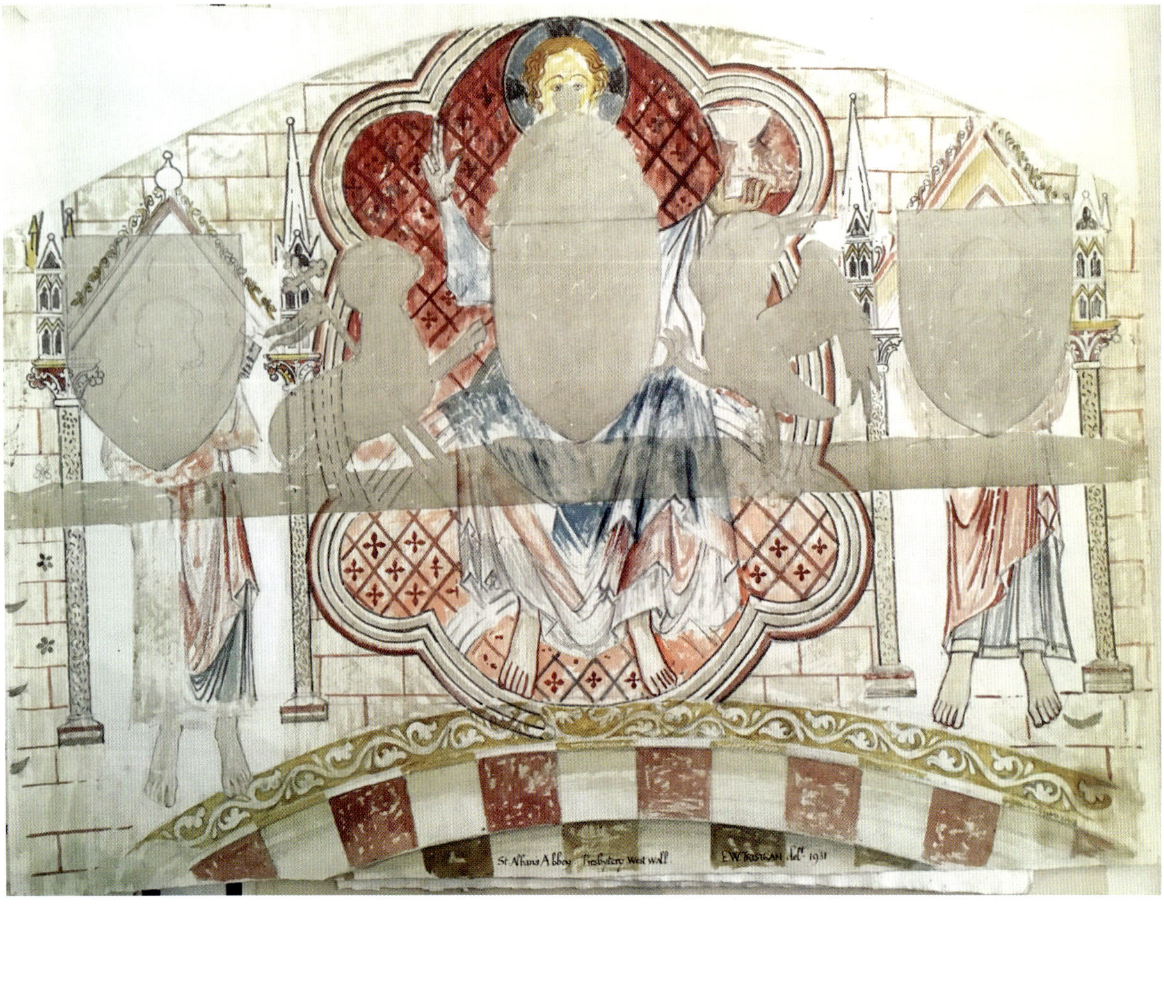

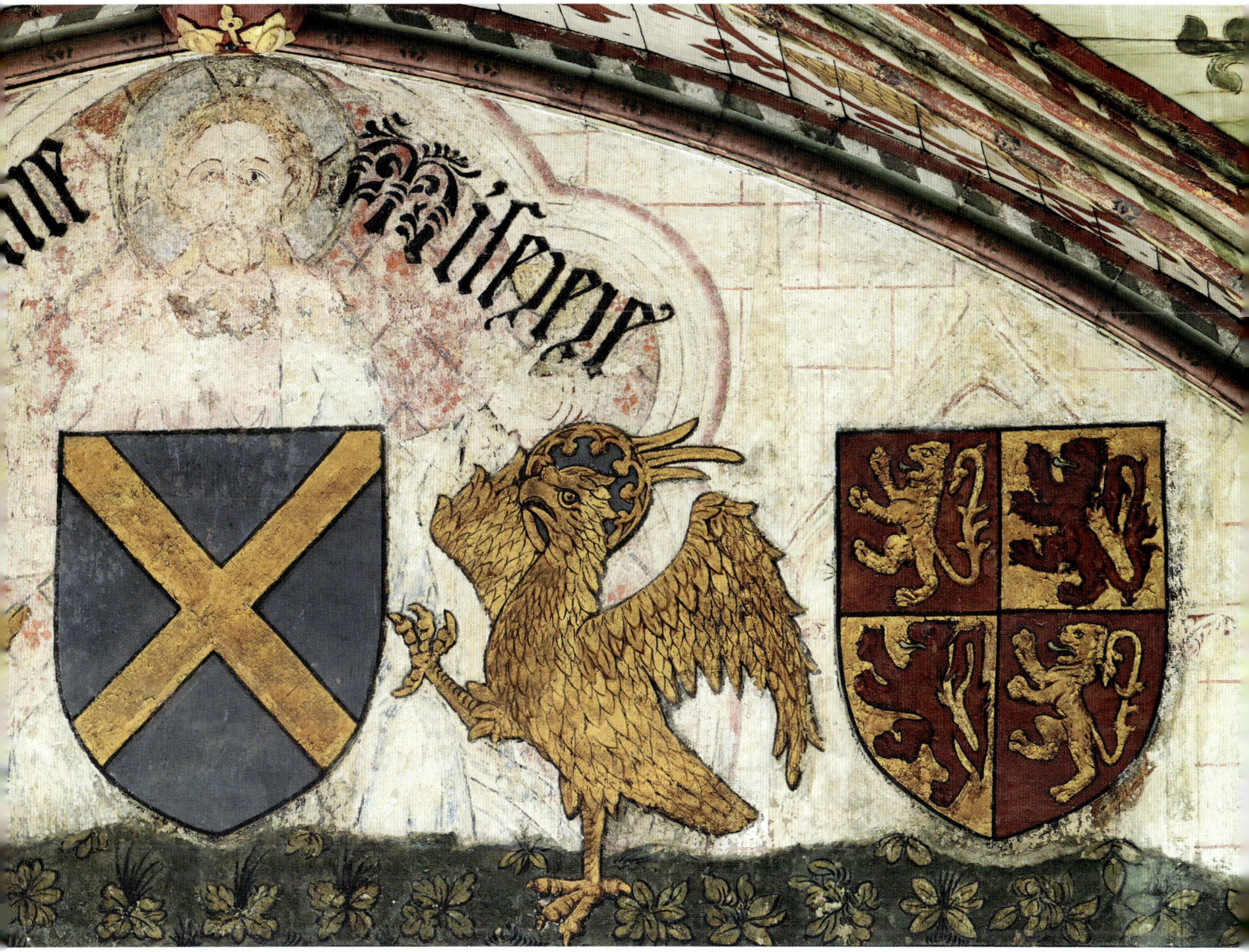

WEST PRESBYTERY WALL *(detail)*

The arrangement of the fifteenth-century inscription, above the shields of Alban and Amphibalus and the eagle of Abbot John Wheathampstead, appears deliberately to avoid obscuring the face of Christ from the earlier image, suggesting that it was incorporated into the repainting of the wall in order to preserve it.

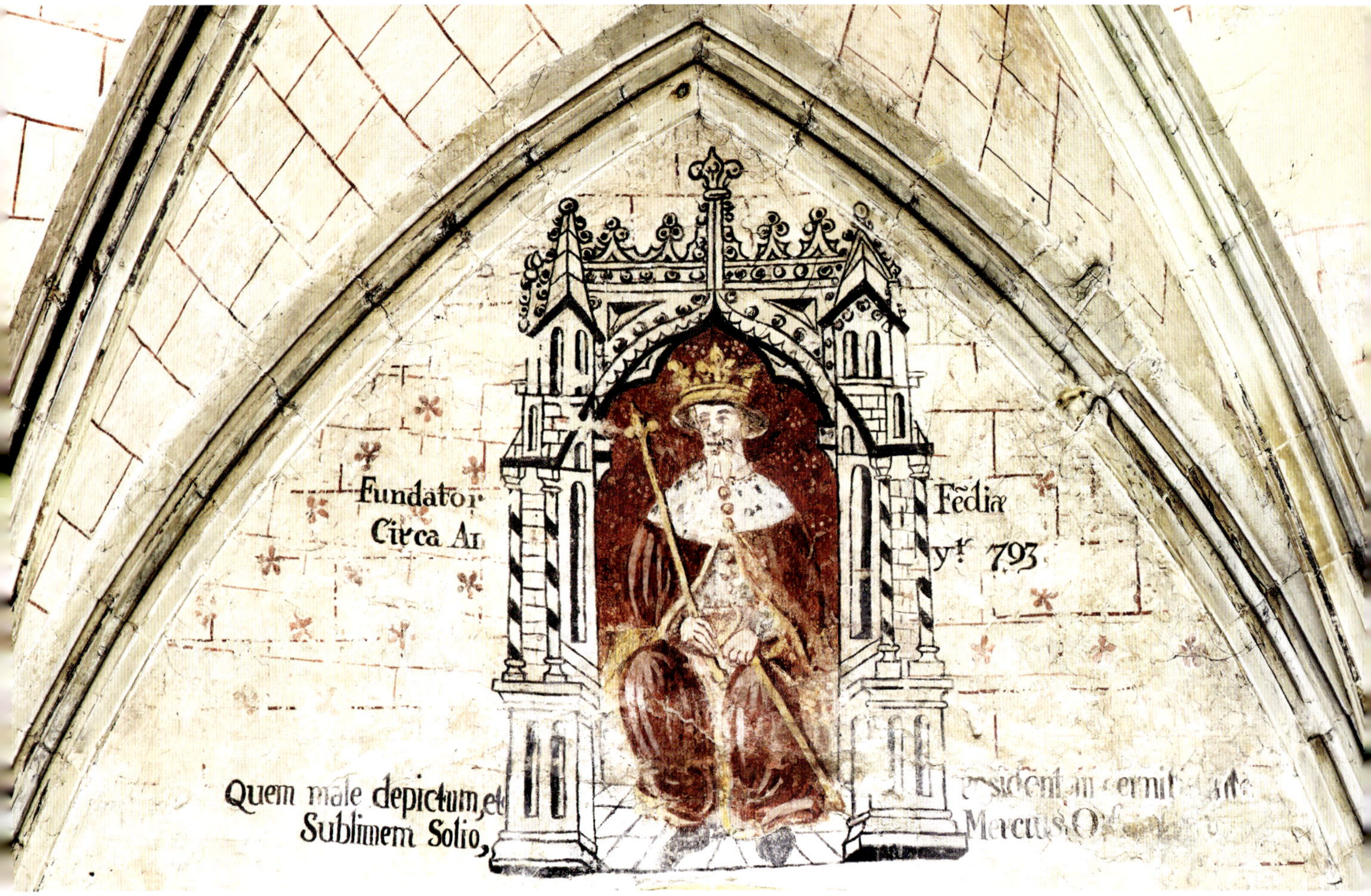

KING OFFA ENTHRONED

The figure of King Offa, founder of St Albans Abbey, is painted high up in the presbytery on the wall that marks the junction of the eleventh-century aisle and the rebuilding work after 1257. He holds a sceptre and sits beneath an ogee arch with pinnacles and shafts supported on bases. The figure itself may date to the early sixteenth century and bears comparison with those in the Garter Book compiled by Sir Thomas Wriothesley, *c.* 1530.[89] The painting was known to a number of eighteenth-century travel writers including Daniel Defoe, who recorded an accurate transcription of the Latin inscriptions in his *Tour thro' the whole Island of Britain of 1724–7*. They read *'Fundator Ecclesiae circa annum 793. Quem male depictum et residentem cernitis alt[o] Sublimem solio, MERCIUS OFFA fuit'* (The founder of the church about 793. Whom you see poorly represented high up on a tall throne, was Offa the Mercian). The statement *'male depictum'*, often literally translated by earlier writers as 'badly painted', may well refer to the image's poor state of conservation by the seventeenth century and its antiquity.

During conservation two layers of paint were noted beneath the figure. The first depicts masonry blocks and was painted soon after the vault was built, the second replaced it with cinquefoil flowers in the fourteenth century. Many repairs were carried out in the nineteenth century, including the partial rewriting of the inscription, probably based on earlier transcriptions. Offa's face and hair were also substantially repainted; the buttons appropriate for his doublet now appear painted over his ermine cape; and the folds of his cloak (sometimes mistaken for a sword) run over a nineteenth-century infill made by the restorer, who left his crude initials 'MN', like a graffito, between the two shafts on the left-hand side of the throne.

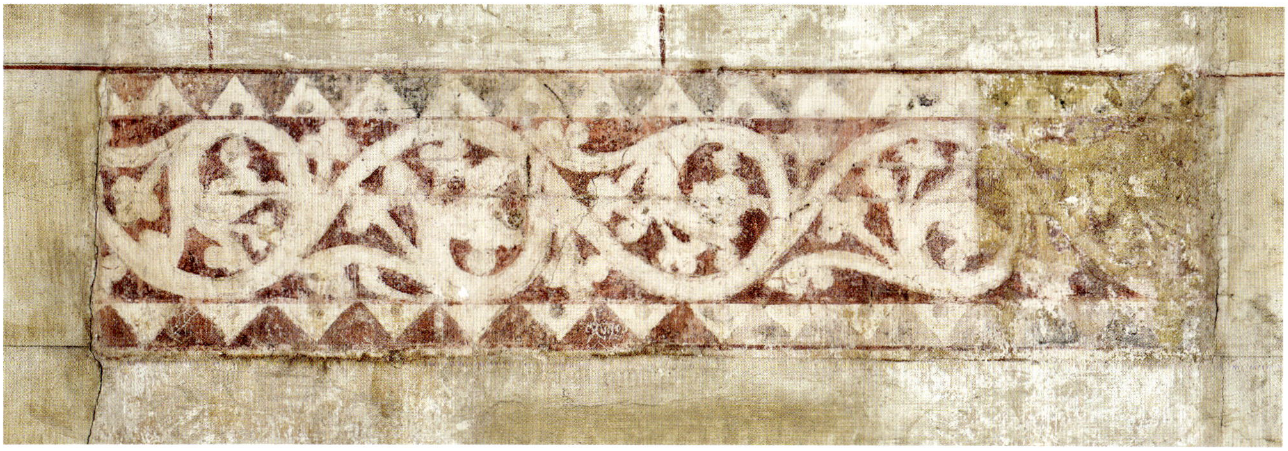

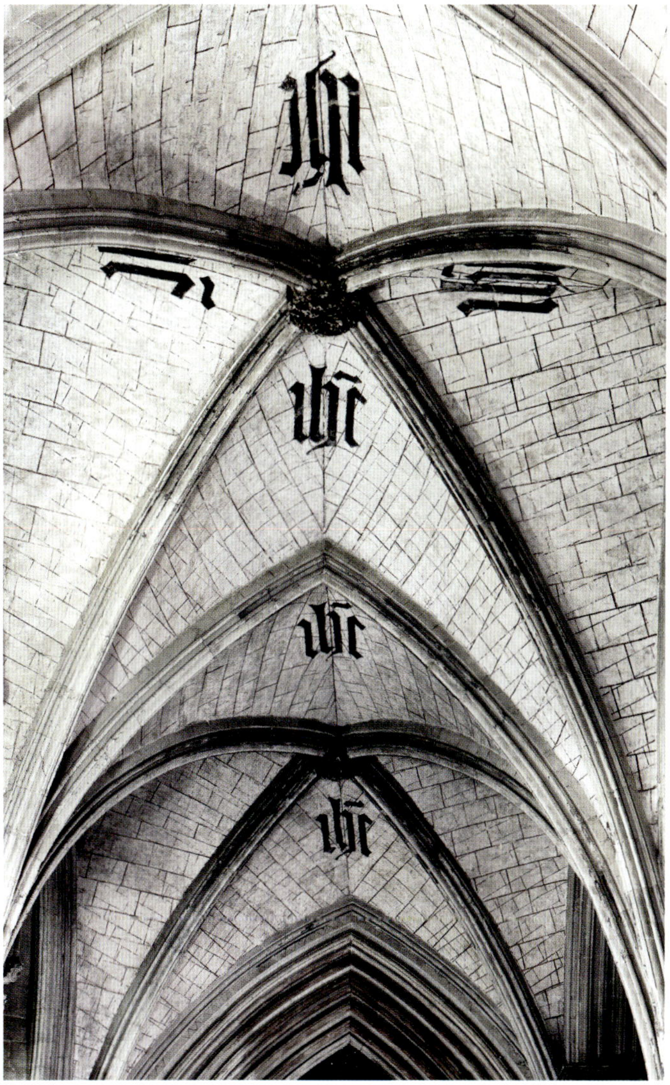

DECORATIVE FRAMING BAND

This small fragment from the south-west wall is all that remains of the painting in the presbytery, after the rebuilding in 1257 prompted by the appearance of cracks in the walls. It consists of a running stiff-leaf scroll enclosed within a sawtooth border and may have continued above the dado level around the whole space. Traces of the original plain imitation ashlar block design, which was initially painted on the whole wall, can be seen in the centre of the design. The lines of the blocks do not match the pattern on the rest of the wall, which is a restoration. Above the scroll work, evidence of further painting can be discerned in the form of a segment of a large circle.

VAULT WITH SACRED MONOGRAM

The simple quadripartite vaults of the north aisle of the presbytery were probably completed during the abbacy of John of Maryns (1302–08). Like most of the wall surfaces in the building, they are decorated with thin red lines to imitate blocks of finely cut stone. The sacred monogram IHS has been painted on top of this design, probably in the fifteenth or early sixteenth century. This monogram, which is an abbreviation of the name of Christ in Latin (*Ihesus*), was thought to protect the building and those in it from danger, as well as designating the area as special in relation to other parts of the building.

SHRINE OF ST ALBAN

We know that by 1129 St Alban's relics were translated (that is, placed in a new shrine) behind the high altar. The relics of St Amphibalus were discovered at Redbourn, Hertfordshire, in 1177 and brought to the abbey in 1178, and new shrines were made for both sets of relics under Abbot Simon (1166–83).[90] We also know that Amphibalus's relics were moved later, under Abbot William of Trumpington, to a place on the north side of the nave. Matthew Paris tells us that the rebuilding of the east end of the abbey was partly dictated by the discovery in 1257 of cracks in the presbytery wall. However, the almost simultaneous discovery of what was believed to be the grave of St Alban at the east end of the church suggests that the need for improvements to the east end of the church was an ongoing concern before the cracks appeared. The old Romanesque apses were demolished soon after, and what is now known as the chapel of St Alban was constructed.

St Alban's shrine appears to have rested originally in the apse of the old Romanesque building, with the high altar in its current position to the west of it. The high screen that now obscures the view into the chapel was not installed until the abbacy of William of Wallingford from 1476. Two altars were placed on the north and south side of the original apse, dedicated to St Oswin (north) and St Wulfstan (south). That on the north was later dedicated to St Hugh (where the Morrow or morning Mass was held) and known as the altar of the relics, while that on the south became the altar of the salutation. Abbot John of Maryns is recorded as having moved and adorned the *'tumba'* (tomb) of Alban, and the current shrine base stands in its original early fourteenth-century position.[91] Like that of St Amphibalus, it was broken into pieces during the Reformation and used as rubble infill for the truncated east end of the church. The fragments were recovered during building works in 1872 and the present shrine base is made up from the pieces that survived, often with substantial amounts of paint remaining.[92] Much of the original carving, which displays scenes of the saint's martyrdom (west face) and scourging (east face), has survived, and the whole presents a rare survival of micro-architecture from the height of the so-called Decorated period in England.

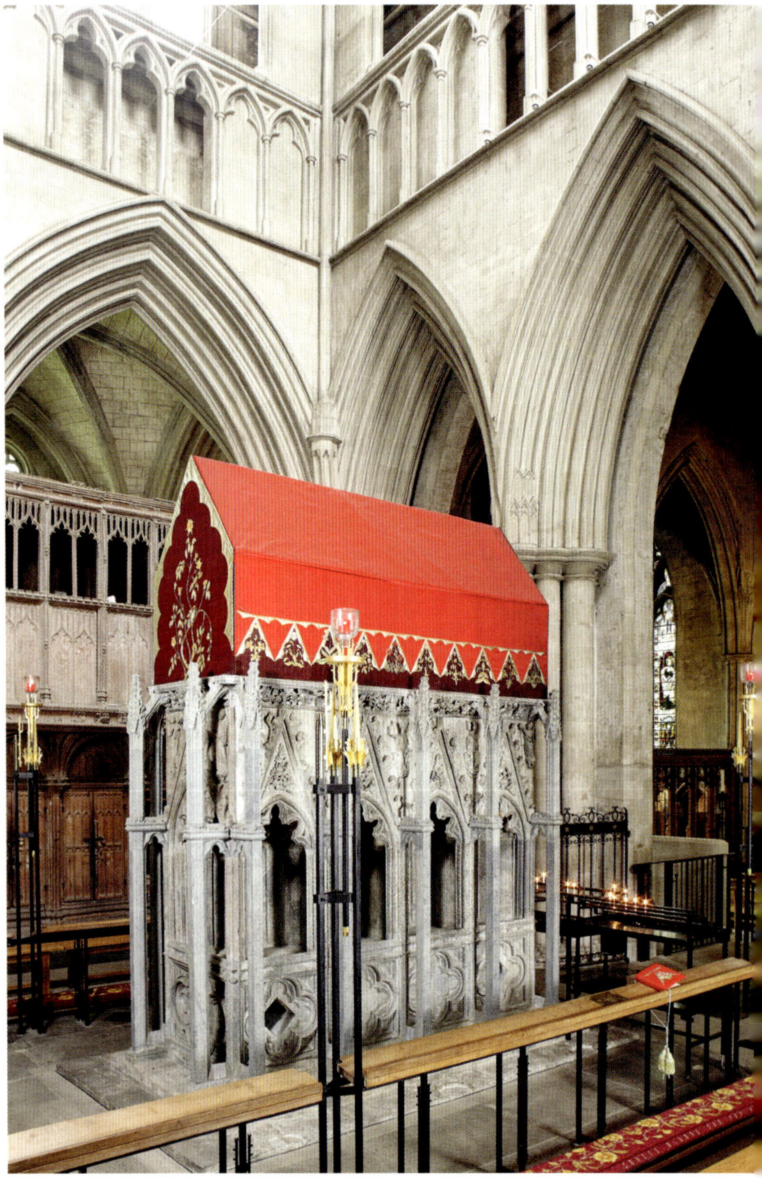

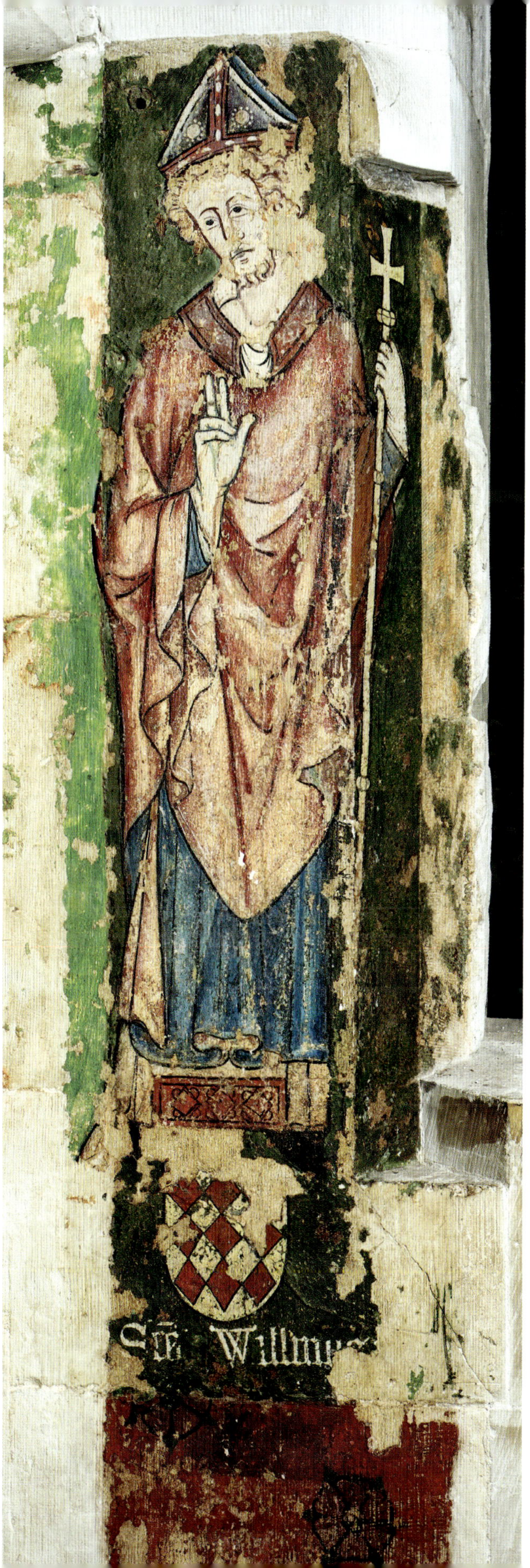

'ST WILLIAM OF YORK'

This figure, originally of a bishop, from the altar of the relics in St Alban's chapel, is one of the most important wall paintings to have survived anywhere in England. It was discovered in 1847 by the rector of St Albans, Dr Henry J.B. Nicholson, when the 'large arches ... forming the east wall of the parish church ... [were] disencumbered'.[93] Now isolated on the left-hand side of the north-east pier of the chapel, it is painted in a sophisticated layering technique using an oil medium. The drawing of the face recalls work in the Westminster Psalter (*c.* 1250), but the drapery reflects that of English illuminated manuscripts from the late thirteenth century.[94] The image formed part of a long, low reredos or retable, the rest of which was probably made of wood. Originally dedicated to St Oswin, the altar was converted into that of St Hugh by the thirteenth century. In *c.* 1428 John Amundesham noted: 'The rest of the relics of the monastery were reverently placed, by the care of brother Robert Trunch [*c.* 1380], in the altar of St Hugh, in divers lockers, plainly secured with locks and keys and bands of iron.'

The figure was altered in the fifteenth century, when the crook-headed crosier of a bishop was converted to the cross appropriate for an archbishop, although it still lacks the pallium, which the later artist has not painted in (cf detail on p. 69). At the same time the Fitzwilliam shield and the inscription *'Scs William'* was painted below the figure, completing its conversion into an image of St William of York (died 1154, canonised 1227). This may have been done after the first battle of St Albans (1455), when Richard, Duke of York was victorious.

The bishop is wearing episcopal gloves and a jewelled mitre, shaded on the front with purple and behind with light blue. His red chasuble is topped by an amice with embroidered apparels visible as a collar. Beneath, the folds of a blue dalmatic can be seen above a white alb with its embroidered orphrey (decorative band) of three pierced quatrefoils on a red ground. A retable of this date would normally have had the Crucifixion or a figure of Christ at its centre. The saint to whom the altar was dedicated could have been placed close to the centre of the composition but such saints are sometimes placed at the extremities, as on the Westminster Retable, and so this image may represent the bishop St Hugh of Lincoln, to whom the altar of the relics was dedicated after his canonisation in 1220.

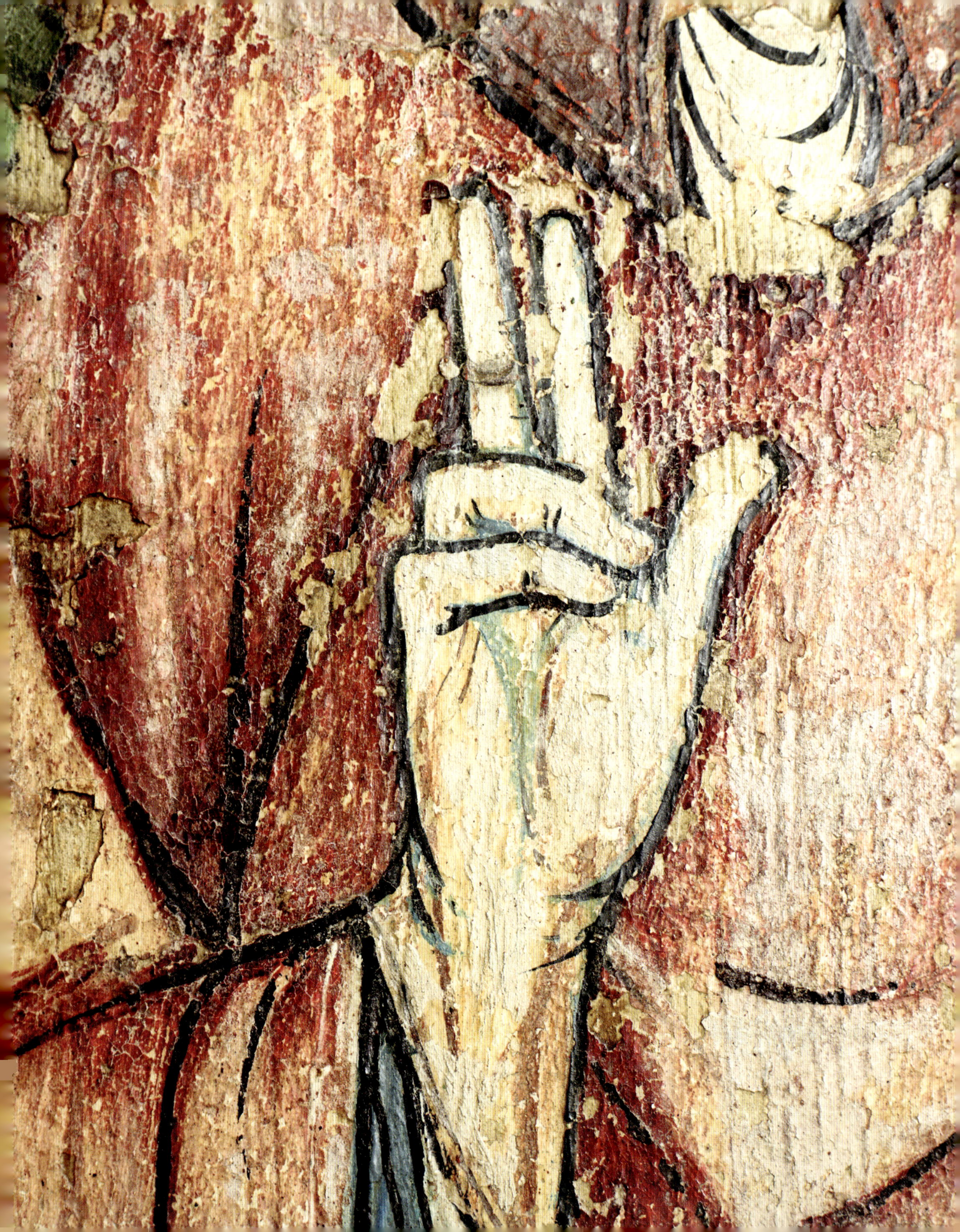

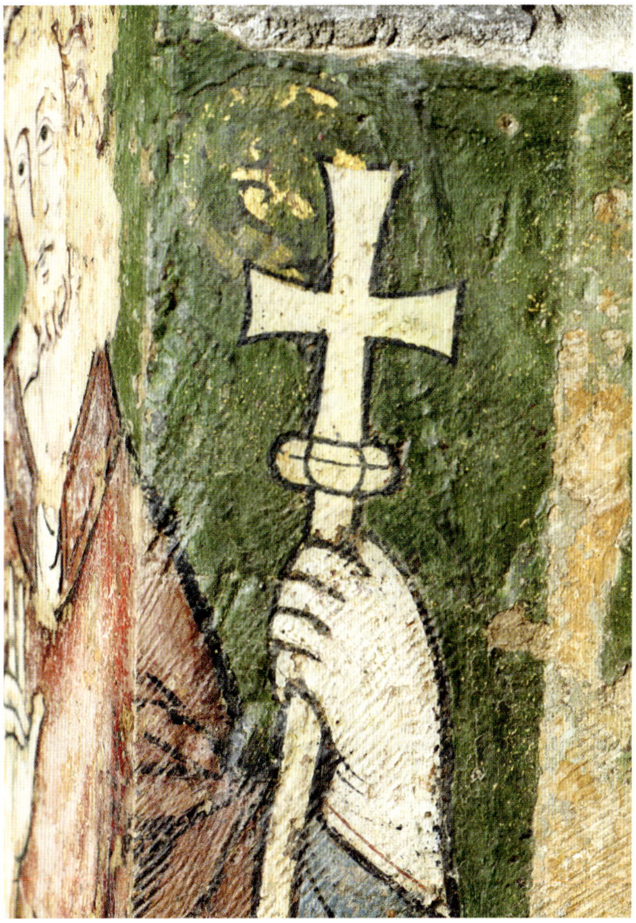

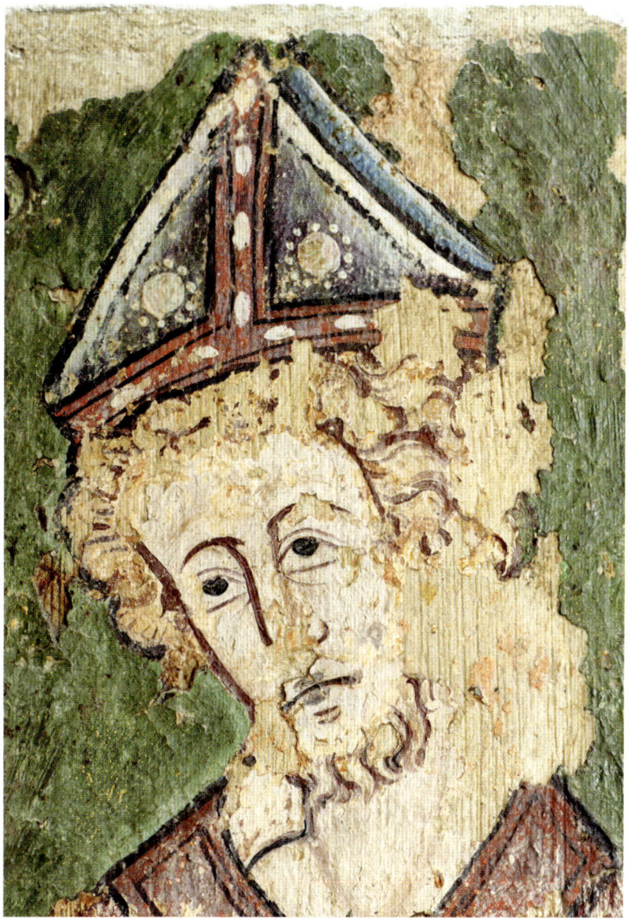

'ST WILLIAM OF YORK' *(details)*

During conservation in 1992–93, the sophistication of the techniques used to paint this figure were fully revealed. A layer of limewash was used to even out the surface of the stone and provide a reflective surface, and further layers of underpaint then applied. The head and the blue drapery were given a ground of red earth pigment, warming the tones of the colours used in the final layers, which were delicately added using an oil medium. Yellow earth was utilised under the original green background, as well as in parts of the red drapery, enhancing the intensity of both colours. Underneath the gilded crosier, visible to the left of the cross added in the fifteenth century, natural vermillion mixed with yellow ochre was used to enhance the glow of the gold. A variety of colours was used, ranging from red lake to vermillion and azurite blue, as well as malachite green, which was overpainted with synthetic copper green in the fifteenth century. This complex layering system is further enhanced by the use of boiled linseed oil, in this case mixed with pine resin, as a medium to build up translucent layers of colour.

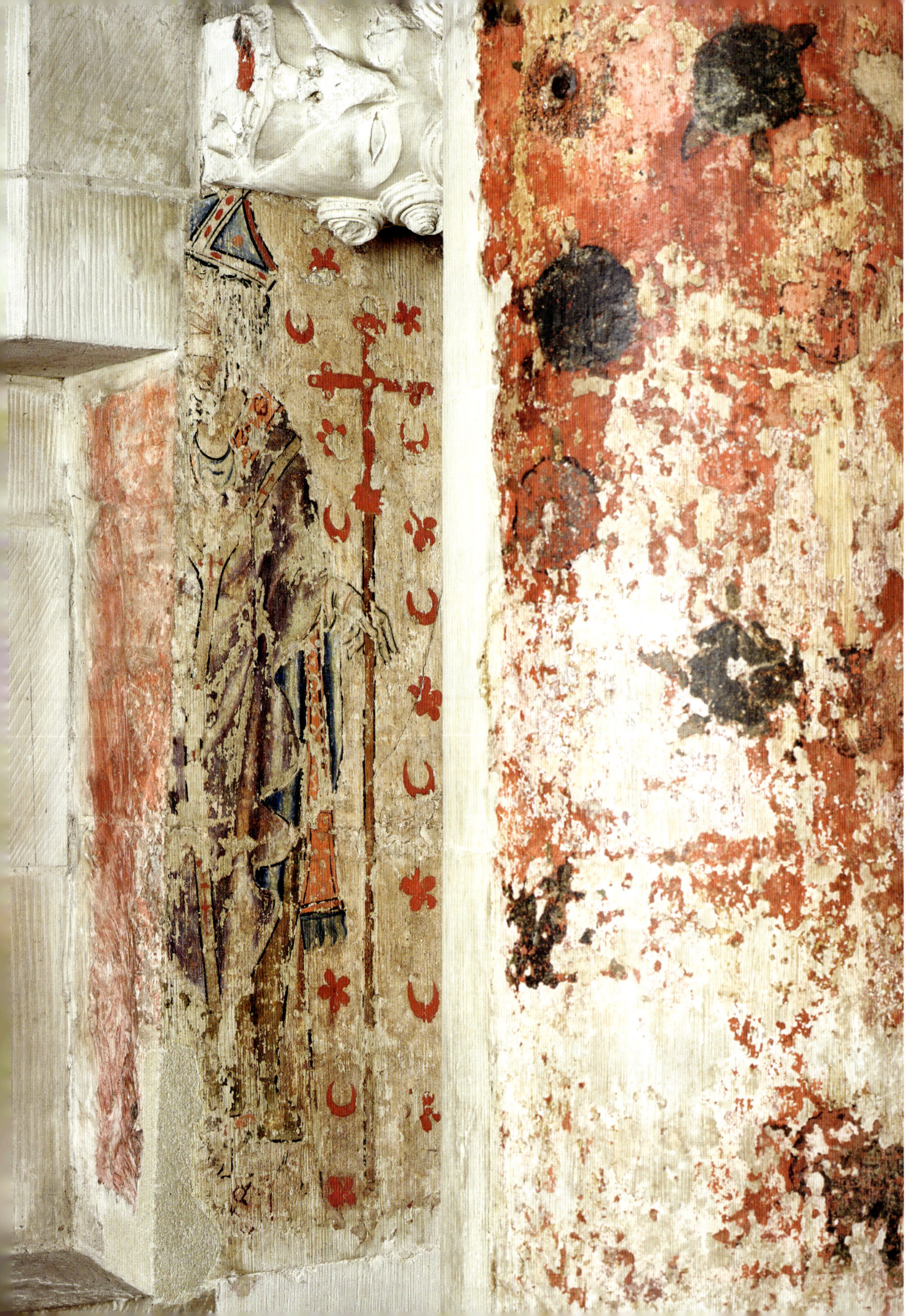

ARCHBISHOP SAINT (THOMAS OF CANTERBURY?)

This figure in the south-east corner of St Alban's shrine chapel is usually assumed to be of the same date as the bishop saint, later converted to St William of York, on the north side, but both technical and stylistic analysis of this painting suggests that it was painted in the fourteenth rather than the last quarter of the thirteenth century.

The archbishop's mitre is partly obscured by an inserted corbel head and only one of his eyes is now visible. The azurite blue of his mitre is lightened with lead white and matches the lining of his chasuble and the fringe of his maniple. The light purple of the chasuble itself is created out of a mixture of red lead and azurite, while both red lead and natural vermillion are used for the crozier, set against a pattern of red crescents and stars. The figure wears an archbishop's white pallium, marked out with red crosses, and an embroidered orange maniple. Unlike the figure of St William, where a methodical layering is used, all these colours were mixed and applied in one layer, making full use of the oil-based medium and the extra translucency of the white lead ground.

The corbel heads inserted to form brackets on the north and south altars of the chapel display evidence of the red paint that sometimes overlays the original painting. This red background covered with rosettes was probably added when the monk Robert de Trunch paid for embellishments to the altars, *c.* 1380, very probably at the same time that the timber watching loft was built, *c.* 1380–1400. It appears that the canopy of the watching loft was mirrored by similar canopies over the two altars, and the ghost of their wooden frame is marked by the angle of the surviving red paint.[95] The figure could be any English archbishop saint but may possibly represent St Thomas Becket, since images of him were depicted elsewhere in the abbey.

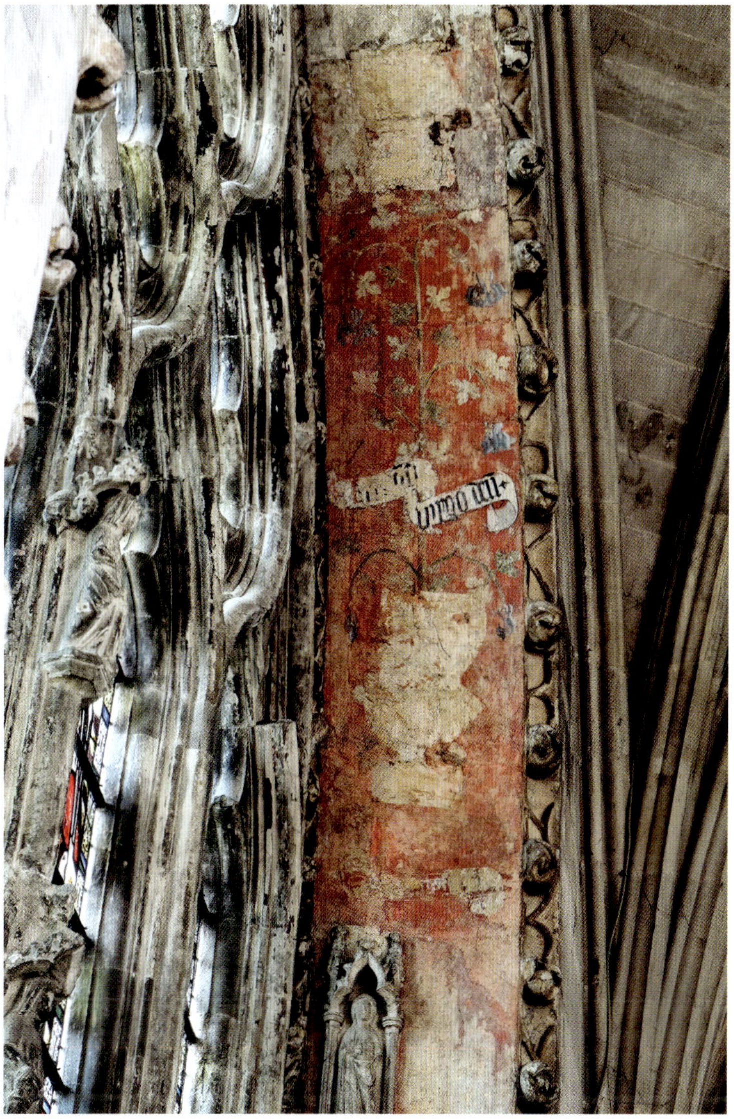

LADY CHAPEL

Under Abbot John of Wheathampstead, the splays of the late thirteenth-century windows in the Lady Chapel were repainted with vases and sprouting vines. One of the inscriptions (still legible in the seventeenth century) referred to the ancestry of the Virgin and her fruitfulness: '*Dulce pluit manna partum dum protulit Anna / Dulcius ancilla dum Christus crevit in ilia*' (manna rained sweetly when Anna gave birth / while Christ grew in that sweeter maid). This responds to the earlier sculpture in the mullion of the window (*c.* 1308–15) that depicts the Virgin and St Anne.[96]

CRUCIFIXION

Humphrey, Duke of Gloucester obtained a licence to build a chantry chapel next to the shrine of St Alban in 1441, and generously endowed it in 1443 with money from the priory of St Nicholas in Pembroke. The chronicler Richard Fox, a lay brother at St Albans, states that the duke was buried in a vault that was made for him during his lifetime.[97] He died in February 1447, shortly after his arrest in Bury St Edmunds for allegedly plotting against his nephew, King Henry VI,[98] which may account for the lack of a tomb chest or reredos within the chapel. He was indeed buried in a lead coffin in the vault beneath the empty chapel, however, and the wall painting on its east wall is one of the most beautiful and iconographically complex images in the abbey. It depicts the Crucifixion, with four cups placed beneath the five bleeding wounds of Christ. The remains of a hand holding a scroll, which once read *'Blessyd Lord have mercy on me'*, probably belonged originally to an image of the duke, painted on the north wall of the narrow vault.

The Crucifixion image probably refers to the popular votive mass of the Five Wounds of Christ.[99] According to the rubric in the Sarum missal, Pope Boniface VIII (1294–1303) was instructed by the archangel Gabriel to ratify the mass so that 'whatsoever tribulation a man shall find himself in this world, if he shall have procured this office to be said five times by a priest for himself, without doubt he shall be delivered from it ... if it be said on behalf of the soul of a deceased person, directly after it has been said completely, that is to say, five times, that soul shall be freed from punishment'.

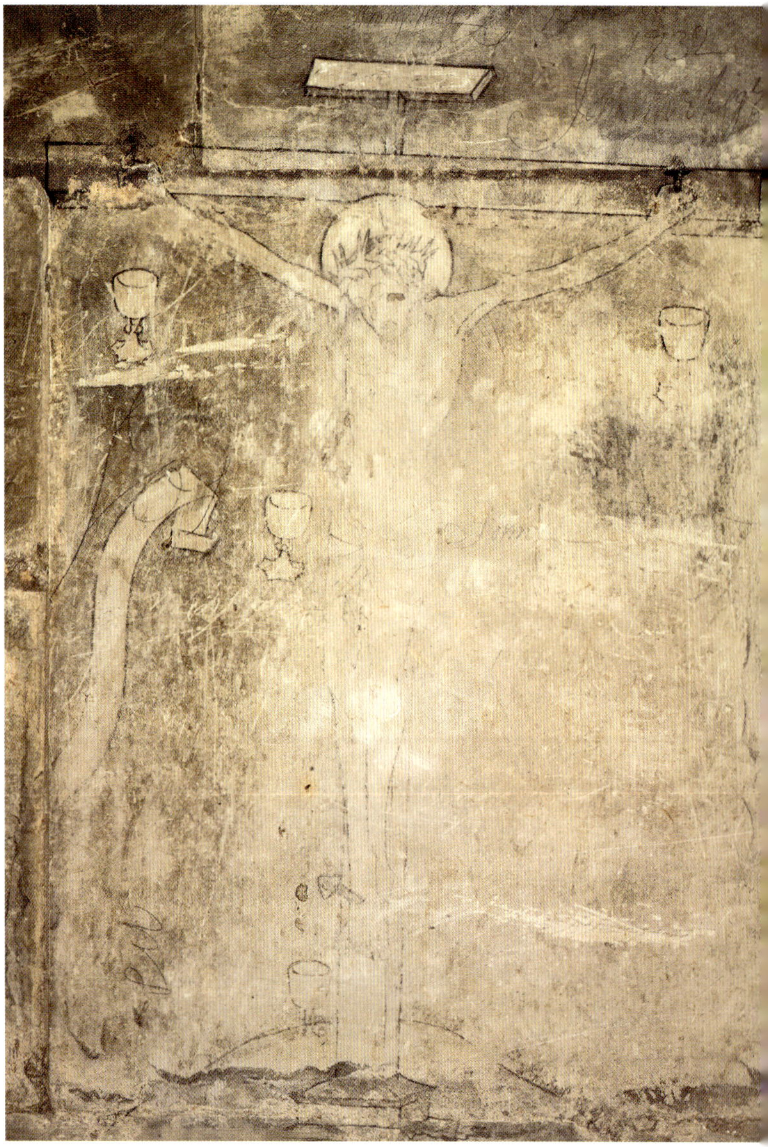

Cups to catch the blood of Christ at the Crucifixion, usually held by angels, are also seen in Giotto's work at the Arena Chapel in Padua (1303–05), and on the shutters of the altarpiece at Klosterneuburg Abbey, Vienna (*c.* 1331), but not beneath the feet of Christ.[100] The Crucifixion in the Lytlington Missal, Westminster (1383–84), is the earliest surviving English example to show angels with cups at all five wounds and this becomes a common iconography in English fifteenth-century alabasters.[101] The emphasis on the blood of Christ in Humphrey's prayerbook (see opposite) suggests he may have given instructions for this painting to be executed.

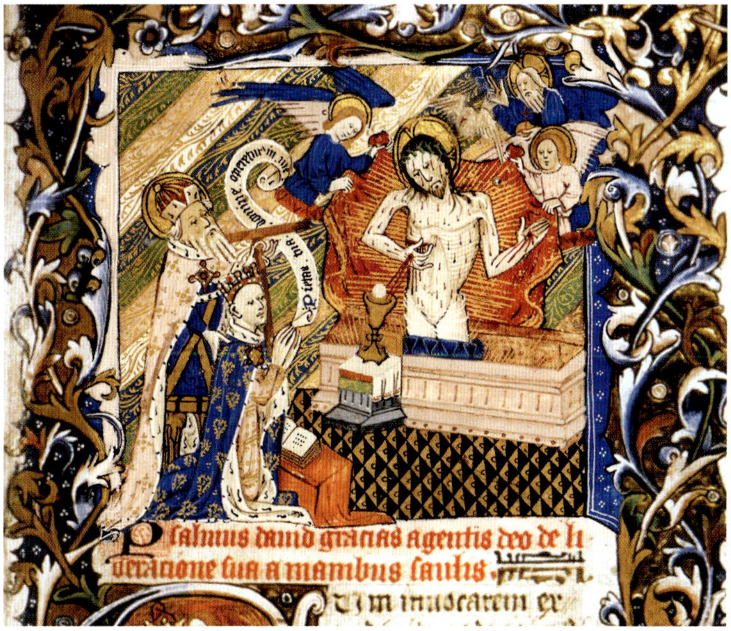

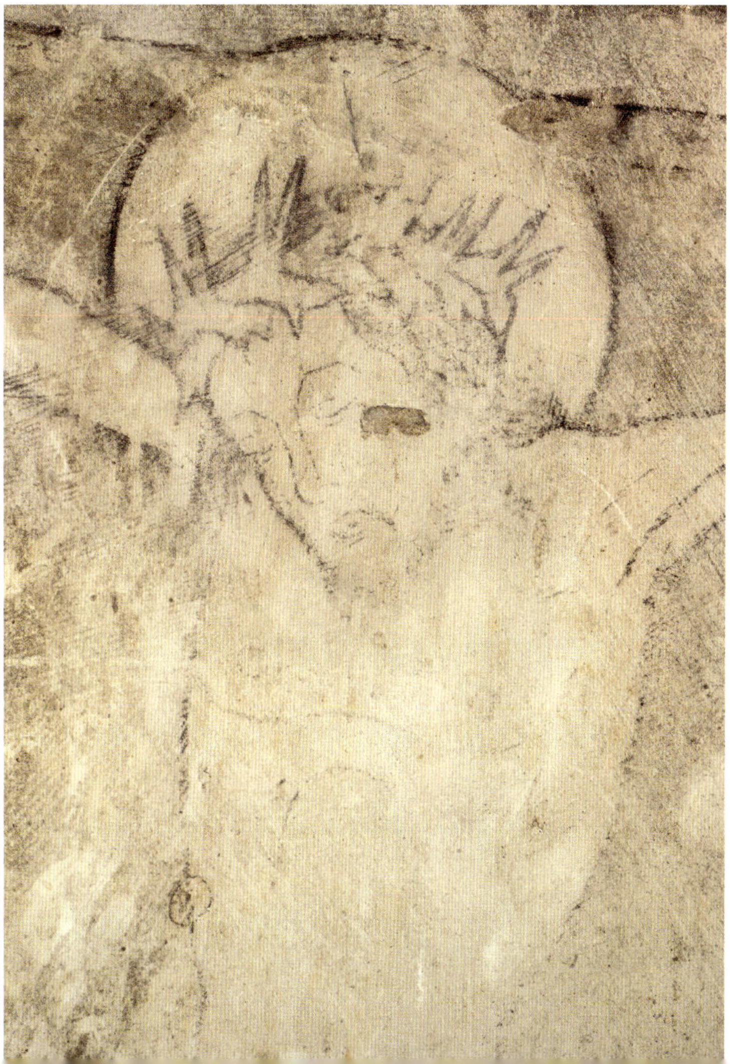

ST ALBAN PRESENTING HUMPHREY, DUKE OF GLOUCESTER TO THE MAN OF SORROWS TRINITY

Humphrey of Gloucester's devotion to St Alban was inspired by his friendship with Abbot John of Wheathampstead, whom he met as a young man at Oxford University. He later became a patron of writers and poets such as John Lydgate and John Capgrave (died 1464) and left his library to what became the Bodleian Library. In his highly personalised prayerbook, Humphrey is shown kneeling at a *prie dieu* (prayer desk) as a member of the abbey confraternity, presented by St Alban himself. The saint is dressed in a heraldic surcoat, armour and exotic hat, in the role of the fictionalised knight and 'Steward of England' created by the monk–chronicler Thomas of Walsingham (see p. 60). The imagery of the Man of Sorrows emerging from the tomb as part of the Trinity, with St Alban carrying the T-shaped cross or *tau*, symbol of the instruments of the passion, is in keeping with contemporary devotional practices. The blood streaming from Christ's wounds falls onto the host itself, shown above a golden chalice placed on a small altar, and the words of the prayer that emerge on a scroll above Humphrey's hands, *'Pietas tua domine operetur in me'* (your mercy, O Lord, has been worked in me), refer to the propitiation achieved at the end of the mass, and specifically to the final prayers said by the priest to the Trinity.

CRUCIFIXION *(detail)*

When the vault was discovered in 1703, 'visitors' began to scrawl graffiti and rob the body of its parts, so that only a few bones and a skull now remain. Because of the confined space, their presence also caused the paint to peel; all that is left is the beautifully drawn outline, which is testimony to the sensitivity of the artist.

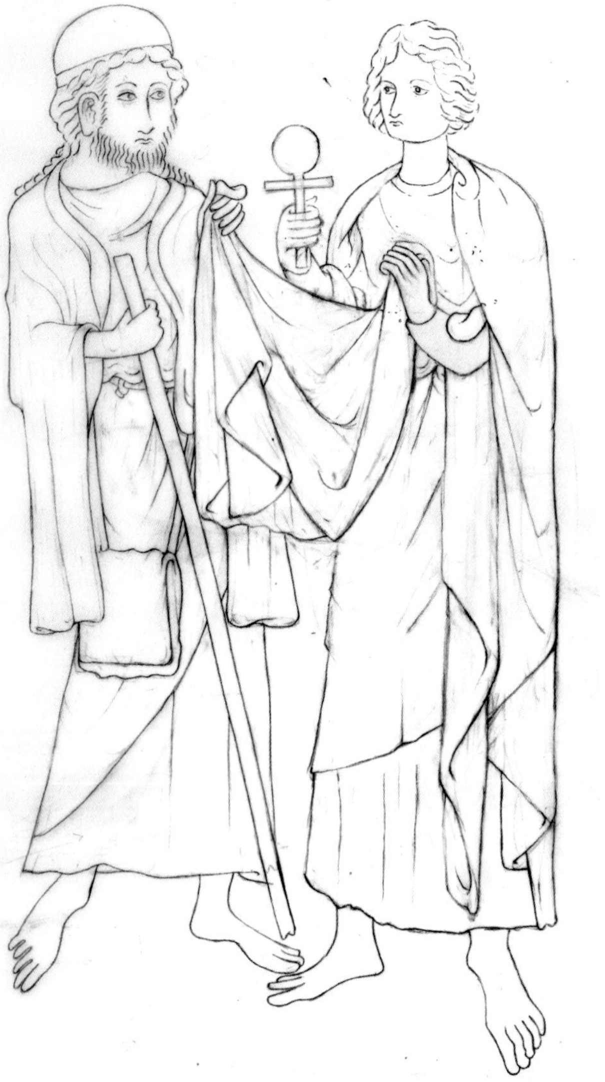

The line drawing which was the end result of the process and which formed the basis for the reconstruction.

The south faces of the Romanesque piers on the north side of the nave provide a perfect canvas for wall paintings, as they are flat surfaces capped by a continuous string course at the level of the arcade impost (the springing point of the arch). Four paintings have survived because they were whitewashed after the dissolution of the monasteries by Henry VIII and were only rediscovered in the nineteenth century (see p. 16). Although damaged, sufficient detail remains to identify them as Sts Christopher, Thomas Becket, Sitha and a narrative scene of Sts Alban and Amphibalus (p. 46). The importance of these monumental images, the only ones of their type to survive from medieval England, has been diminished by defacement (see p. 42), but enough of their outlines are visible for a reconstruction to be attempted. In 2018, with the aid of a National Lottery Heritage Fund grant, together with a grant from the Friends of St Albans Abbey, the cathedral launched an ambitious project to create a digital projection, using photography and new artwork based on an archaeological reconstruction of the originals. The aim of this was to enhance and re-colour the paintings without damage, so that they can again play their original role within the modern cathedral.

Archaeological illustrator Craig Williams was tasked with investigating the paintings and providing digital reconstructions for projection. As well as the high-resolution photography commissioned from Angelo Hornak, further detailed photographs in raking light were also taken to better understand the areas where important features had survived. In order to ensure that an accurate image would be projected, measurements were taken and each layer of intervention was documented archaeologically, starting with the latest activity on the surface and going back in successive stages to the original paint surface.

The earliest of the monumental paintings is that on the fourth painted pier, depicting Sts Alban and Amphibalus. This was also the most challenging because of the nature of the different periods of defacement, both deliberate and accidental, and the resulting attempts at conservation (p. 16). In order to create the digital image of each painting, a carefully staged process was followed to record and interpret the findings.

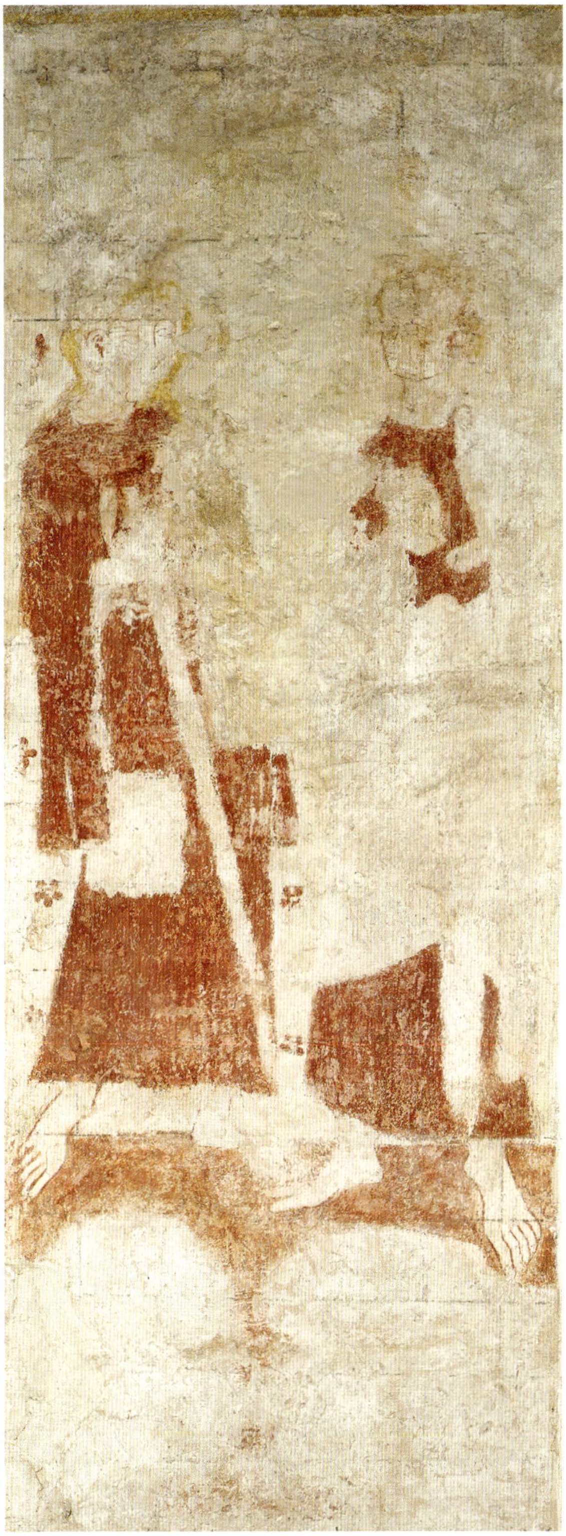

The pier painting of Sts Alban and Amphibalus as it looks today.

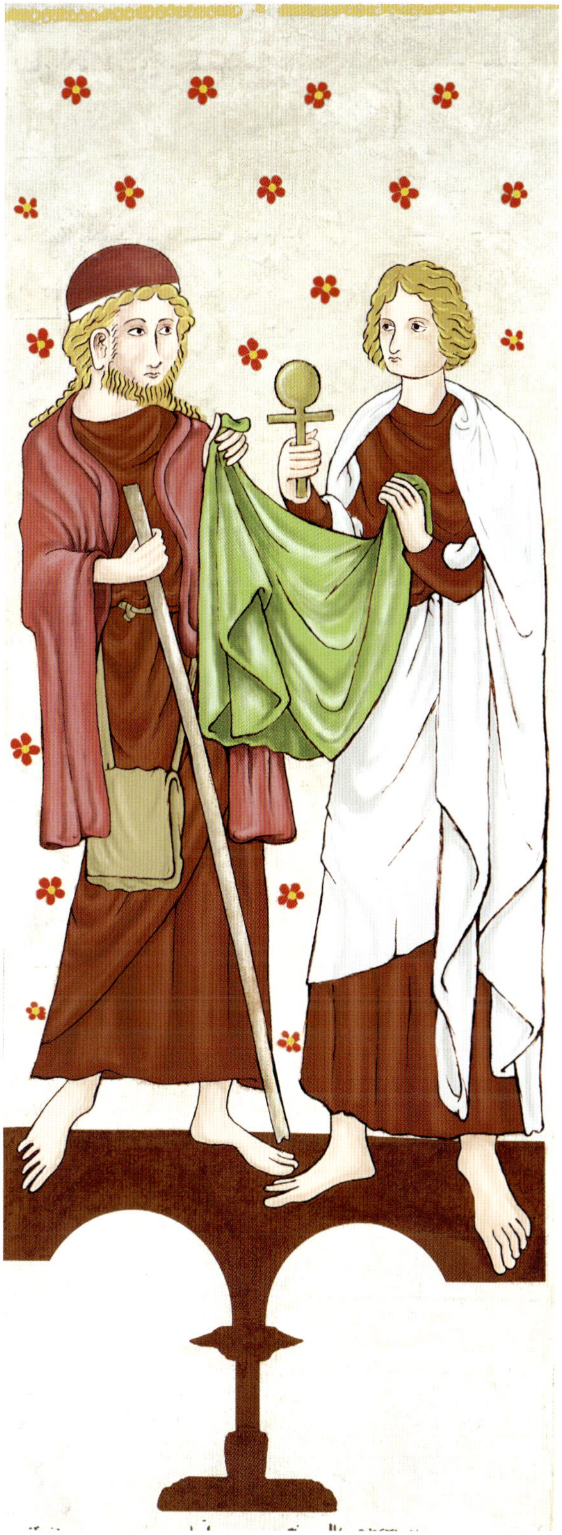

The reconstructed painting of Sts Alban and Amphibalus, based on the detailed analysis and investigative process described and illustrated overleaf.

Fig. 1

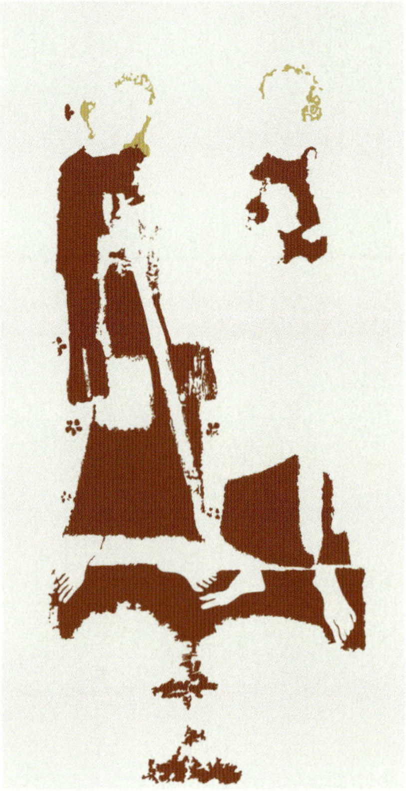

Fig. 2

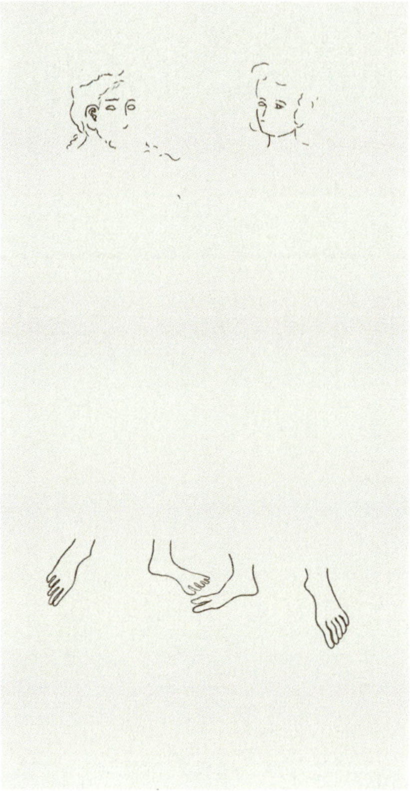

Fig. 3

STAGE 1 (see Fig. 1)

The first stage documented areas where the limewash ground had been completely removed and incisions had been made, in the form of deep deliberate criss-cross scratches (indicating defacement) and lighter shallow scratches (indicating the nineteenth-century cleaning). It was noted that the deeper criss-cross scratches also occurred on the other three paintings exactly where the faces would have been on each figure. The faces of Sts Alban and Amphibalus were not defaced but the same deep incisions were observed, at the same height as the heads of the other saints. This suggests that Alban and Amphibalus were painted over prior to the dissolution of the monasteries, probably after the shrine of St Amphibalus was moved further east in the abbey in the fourteenth century (p. 47). There can be no doubt that, if they had been visible to the iconoclasts of the sixteenth or seventeenth centuries, their faces would have also been scratched out. It seems that another figure was painted over them, probably when the image of St Sitha (on the third painted pier) was executed, and this later painting was lost during the over-zealous cleaning of the nineteenth century. Traces of paint and incisions at the centre of the painting suggest a belt that belonged to the lost figure.

STAGE 2 (see Figs 2 and 4)

The pigment was accurately recorded and each colour was separated out in order to produce individual digital layers. This was an important process, as it provided an archaeological record of the current state of the paintings for conservation purposes, and also helped to prevent inaccurate readings of the imagery. Damaged or ambiguous elements within a block of colour were also noted at this stage in order to identify areas where an expected iconographical element, such as a saint's attribute, may have been depicted. In the case of Alban and Amphibalus, it confirmed the presence of a cloak, and possibly a cross, in the centre of the composition.

STAGE 3 (see Figs 3, 4 and 5)

The more detailed paintwork, comprising the outlines of facial features where visible, and any text elements, were recorded for each painting. These were then related to the earlier observations of scratches and defacement. Unlike the other monumental paintings on the nave piers, evidence of the initial drawing of the faces was visible in the case of both Alban and Amphibalus.

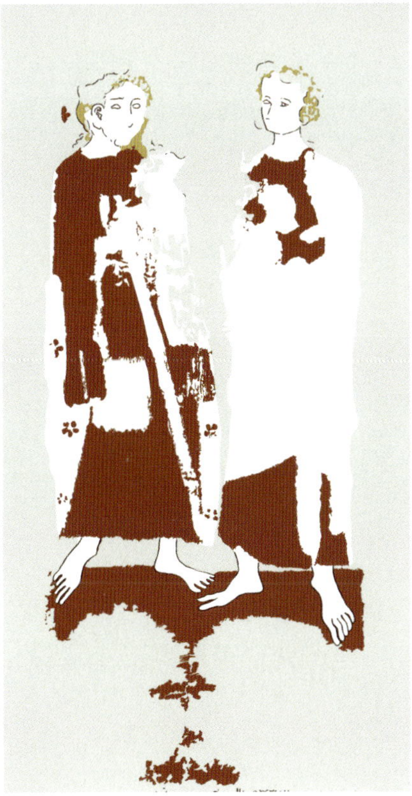

Fig. 4

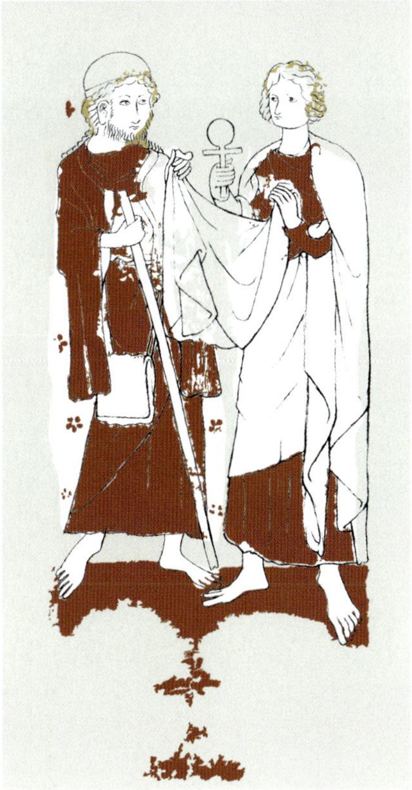

Fig. 5

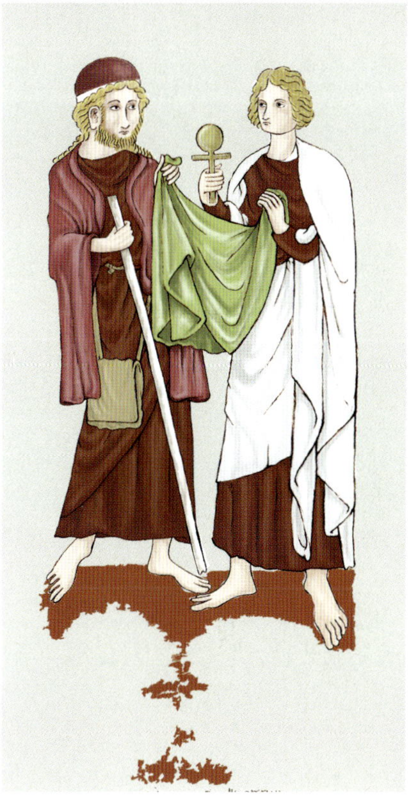

Fig. 6

STAGE 4 (see Figs 5 and 6)

The information from a combined drawing was assessed in the light of evidence from contemporary painting and manuscript illumination. The missing elements were then restored by continuing lines that would once have joined and by filling in areas of colour that were once unified. In the case of the scene showing Alban and Amphibalus, the near contemporary narrative image provided by Matthew Paris in his *Life of St Alban* (p. 47), of the saint receiving the cloak and cross from Amphibalus, suggested that the large area at the centre of the painting was indeed a cloak and probably also included the cross, which is no longer visible.

STAGE 5 (see line drawing on p. 74)

A pencil drawing was then produced, taking account of all the features noted in the digital photographs, as well as the various layers of investigation and iconographical observations from contemporary sources.

STAGE 6 (see reconstructed painting on p. 75)

The digital reproduction of the scene depicting Sts Alban (right) and Amphibalus, identified by his attributes of staff and pilgrim's satchel (left), has been enhanced by colour which references the pigments seen on surviving paintings in the immediate vicinity of St Albans and contemporary illuminated manuscripts. The colour has been layered in order to create a clear, bright image that reflects the impression of the original. Clear evidence of the cloak of St Alban was found at the centre of the image but it was also decided to introduce the annular cross of St Alban (not now visible on the painting), as this was an important relic brought back to the abbey by William of Trumpington. It was introduced by Matthew Paris into the iconography of the scene of the exchange of the cloak of St Amphibalus (*c.* 1240–50) shortly before the wall painting is likely to have been executed (*c.* 1250–70).

BIBLIOGRAPHY

Barron 2007: Caroline M. Barron, 'The travelling saint: Zita of Lucca and England', in *Harlaxton Medieval Studies XV (New Series), Proceedings of the 2003 Harlaxton Symposium: Freedom of Movement in the Middle Ages*, ed. Peregrine Horden (Donington, 2007), pp. 186–202

Beckett 1890: Edmund Beckett, Lord Grimthorpe, *St. Albans Cathedral and its Restoration* (2nd edition, St Albans, 1890)

Biddle 1990: Martin Biddle, 'Remembering St Alban: the site of the shrine and discovery of the twelfth-century Purbeck marble shrine table', in *Alban and St Albans: Roman and Medieval Architecture, Art and Archaeology*, eds. Martin Henig and Phillip Lindley, *British Archaeological Association Conference Transactions*, vol. 24 (2001), pp. 124–61

Biddle 2004: Martin Biddle, 'Amphibalus: cult and shrine', in St Amphibalus Shrine Symposium 28 September 2004 (unpublished report, St Albans, 2004), pp. 6–12

Biddle and Kjølbye-Biddle 1990: Martin Biddle and Birthe Kjolbye-Biddle, 'Early painted wall plaster from St Albans abbey', in *Early Medieval Wall Painting and Painted Sculpture in England*. Based on the proceedings of a symposium at the Courtauld Institute of Art, February 1985, ed. Sharon Cather, David Park and P. Williamson, BAR (1990), pp. 73–78

Binski 1992: Paul Binski, 'The murals in the nave of St Albans abbey', in *Church and City 1000–1500. Essays in Honour of Christopher Brooke*, ed. David Abulafia, Michael Franklin and Miri Rubin (Cambridge, 1992), pp. 249–78

Blindheim 2004: Martin Blindheim, *Gothic Painted Wooden Sculpture in Norway 1220–1350* (Oslo, 2004)

Buckler and Buckler 1847: John Chessell Buckler and Charles Alban Buckler, *A History of the Architecture of the Abbey Church of St. Alban: with Special Reference to the Norman Structure* (London, 1847)

Carter 1813: John Carter, *Some Account of the Abbey Church of St Alban* (London, 1813)

Cheetham 2005: Francis Cheetham, *English Medieval Alabasters: with a Catalogue of the Collection in the Victoria and Albert Museum* (Woodbridge, 2005)

Cherry 1992: John Cherry, *Medieval Craftsmen: Goldsmiths* (London, 1992)

Clark 2001: James G. Clark, 'The St Albans monks and the cult of St Albans', in *Alban and St Albans: Roman and Medieval Architecture, Art and Archaeology*, eds Martin Henig and Phillip Lindley, *British Archaeological Association Conference Transactions*, vol. 24 (2001), pp. 218–30

Clark 2002: James G. Clark, 'Thomas Walsingham reconsidered: books and learning at late-medieval St. Albans', *Speculum*, vol. 77 (2002), pp. 832–60

Coldstream 1990: Nicola Coldstream, *'Cui bono?* The saint, the clergy and the new work at St Albans', in *Medieval Architecture and its Intellectual Context. Studies in Honour of Peter Kidson*, ed. Eric Fernie and Paul Crossley (London and Ronceverte, 1990), pp. 14–149

Davidson 2016: Clifford Davidson, *Studies in Late Medieval Wall Paintings, Manuscript Illuminations, and Texts* (Kalamazoo, 2016)

Duffy 2005: Eamon Duffy, *The Stripping of the Altars: Traditional Religion in England 1400–1580* (2nd edition, New Haven and London, 2005)

Dugdale 1846: William Dugdale, 'St Alban's monastery', in *Monasticon Anglicanum: a New Edition Enriched with a Large Accession of Materials... by John Caley... Henry Ellis... and Bulkeley Bandinel*, vol. 2 (London, 1846), pp. 178–255

Dutschke and Rouse 1989: Consuelo W. Dutschke and Richard H. Rouse, *Guide to Medieval and Renaissance Manuscripts in the Huntington Library* (San Marino, 1989)

Fehrmann 2011: Antje Fehrmann, 'Politics and posterity: English royal chantry provision 1232–1509', *Journal of the British Archaeological Association*, ed. Julian Luxford and John McNeill, vol. 164 (2011), pp. 74–99

Gilbert Scott 1872: George Gilbert Scott, '... how the difficulties with respect to the date of the St. Alban's shrine may be reconciled', *Archaeological Journal*, vol. 29 (1872), pp. 210–11

Giles 1853: *Matthew Paris's English History*, vol. 2, trans. J.A. Giles (London, 1853)

Gill 2000: Miriam Gill, 'The role of images in monastic education: the evidence from wall painting in late medieval England', in *Medieval Monastic Education*, ed. George Ferzoco and Carolyn Muessig (London and New York, 2000), pp. 117–35

Gough 1786: Richard Gough, *Sepulchral Monuments in Great Britain Applied to Illustrate the History of Families, Manners, Habits and Arts, at the Different Periods from the Norman Conquest to the Seventeenth Century*, 2 vols, (London, 1786–96), vol. 2 (London, 1786)

Harrison et al. 2012: Hugh Harrison, John McNeill, Pauline Plummer and Gavin Simpson, 'The presbytery vault at St Albans', *The Antiquaries Journal*, vol. 92 (2012), pp. 245–72

Howard 1993: Helen Howard, 'Workshop practices and identification of hands: gothic wall paintings at St Albans', *The Conservator*, no. 17 (1993), pp. 34–45

Howard 2003: Helen Howard, *Pigments of English Medieval Wall Painting* (London, 2003)

Kelsall 2013: Jane Kelsall, *Humphrey Duke of Gloucester 1391–1447* (2nd edition, St Albans, 2013)

Keyser 1883: Charles E. Keyser, *A List of Buildings in Great Britain and Ireland Having Mural and other Painting Decorations* (London, 1883)

Kjølbye-Biddle 2001: Birthe Kjølbye-Biddle, 'The Alban cross', in *Alban and St Albans: Roman and Medieval Architecture, Art and Archaeology*, eds Martin Henig and Phillip Lindley, *British Archaeological Association Conference Transactions*, vol. 24 (2001), pp. 85–110

Knowles et al. 2008: David Knowles et al., *The Heads of Religious Houses: England and Wales, 1377–1540*, vol. 3 (Cambridge, 2008)

Lawrence 1996: Clifford H. Lawrence, *The Life of St Edmund by Matthew Paris* (Stroud, 1996)

Lethaby 1916: William R. Lethaby, 'English Primitives – Master Walter of Colchester, *The Incomparable Painter*', *c.* 118–1248, and the Master of the Chichester Roundel' *Burlington Magazine*, vol. 29 (1916), pp. 189–91 and 194–96

Lloyd 1873a: Robert Ridgway Lloyd, *Johannes Amundesham, An account of the Altars, Monuments & Tombs Existing A.D. 1428 in Saint Albans Abbey* [extr. from J. Amundesham's *Annales monasterii s. Albani*] tr. with notes by Ridgway Lloyd (St Albans, 1873)

Lloyd 1873b: Robert Ridgway Lloyd, *An Architectural and Historical Account of the Shrines of Saint Alban and Saint Amphibalus in Saint Albans Abbey* (St Albans and Langley, 1873)

Lloyd 1882; Robert Ridgway Lloyd, 'The wall paintings in St Albans abbey', *Archaeological Journal*, vol. 39 (1882)

Luard 1874: Henry R. Luard, ed., *Matthaei Parisiensis, monachi Sancti Albani: Chronica majora* (Rolls Series), 7 vols (London, 1872–84), vol. 2 (London, 1874)

MacCraken 1911: Henry M. MacCraken, *The Minor Poems of John Lydgate: Edited from all Available Manuscripts with an Attempt to Establish the Lydgate Canon*, Part 1 (London and New York, 1911)

McClure and Collins 2008: *Bede: The Ecclesiastical History of the English People*, eds Judith McClure and Roger Collins (Oxford, 2008)

Marks and Payne 1988: Richard Marks and Ann Payne, eds, *British Heraldry from its Origins to c. 1800* (London, 1978)

Meiss 1967: Millard Meiss, *French Painting in the Time of Jean De Berry: The Late Fourteenth Century and the Patronage of the Duke*, 2 vols, vol. 1 (London, 1967)

Michael 2004: Michael A. Michael, *Stained Glass of Canterbury Cathedral* (London, 2004)

Michael 2017: Michael A. Michael, 'A re-evaluation of the wall paintings on the north nave piers of St. Albans abbey: An exercise in stylistic and iconographical analysis', in *Tributes to Adelaide Bennett Hagens. Manuscripts, Iconography, and the Late Medieval Viewer*, eds Pamela A. Patton and Judith K. Golden (Turnhout, 2017), pp. 229–59

Micklethwaite 1872: John T. Micklethwaite, 'The shrine of St Alban', *Archaeological Journal*, vol. 29 (1872), pp. 200–210

Morgan 1982: Nigel J. Morgan, *A Survey of Manuscripts Illuminated in the British Isles, vol. 4, Early Gothic Manuscripts*, vol. 1 (London, 1982)

Morgan 1988: Nigel J. Morgan, *A Survey of Manuscript Illuminated in the British Isles, vol. 4, Early Gothic Manuscripts*, vol. 2 (London, 1988)

Munns 2016: John Munns, *Cross and Culture in Anglo-Norman England: Theology, Imagery, Devotion* (Woodbridge, 2016)

Nicholson 1851: Henry J.B. Nicholson, *The Abbey of Saint Alban. Some Extracts from its Early History and a Description of its Conventual Church* (London, 1870)

North 1976: John D. North, *Richard of Wallingford: An Edition of his Writings with Introductions, English Translation and Commentary*, 3 vols (Oxford, 1976)

O'Keeffe 2000: Patrick O'Keeffe 'Latin inscriptions in St Albans abbey', *The Fraternity and Friends of St Albans Abbey, Occasional Paper*, N.S. no. 7 (St Albans, 2000)

Oman 1932: Charles Oman, 'The goldsmiths of St Albans abbey, during the 12th and 13th centuries', *Transactions of the St Albans and Hertfordshire Architectural and Archaeological Society* (1932), pp. 215–36

Ovrey 1850: Fredric Ovrey (chair), 'Proceedings at the meetings of the Archaeological Institute', *Archaeological Journal*, vol. 7 (1850), pp. 65–403

Owst 1926: Gerald R. Owst, 'A fifteenth-century manuscript in St Albans abbey', *Transactions of the St Albans and Hertfordshire Architectural and Archaeological Society* (1924), pp. 43–59

Page 1898: William T. Page, *St. Alban's Cathedral and Abbey Church*, a Guide (London, 1898)

Page 1899: William T. Page, 'The brasses and indents in St. Albans abbey', *Home Counties Magazine*, vol. 1 (1899), pp. 19–25, 140–61, 241–47 and 329–32

Page 1902: William T. Page, 'The St Albans school of painting (mural and miniature): Part I mural painting', *Archaeologia*, vol. 58 (1902), pp. 1–18

Page 1908: William T. Page, ed., *Victoria County History of the Counties of England: Hertfordshire*, vol. 2 (London, 1908)

Park 1987: David Park, 'Wall painting', in *Age of Chivalry: Art in Plantagenet England 1200–1400*, eds Jonathan J.G. Alexander and Paul Binski (London, 1987)

Perry Lithgow 1992: Perry Lithgow Partnership, 'St Albans Cathedral Nave: Pier 1', *Unpublished Conservation Report*, 1992, pp. 1–2

Preest and Clark 2019: David Preest and James G. Clark (trans.), *The Deeds of the Abbots of St Albans: Gesta Abbatum Monasterii Sancti Albani* (Woodbridge, 2019)

Pridgeon 2008: Eleanor Pridgeon, *Saint Christopher Wall Paintings in English and Welsh Churches c. 1250–c.1500* (Leicester, 2008), p. 204

Pridgeon 2013: Eleanor Pridgeon, 'National and international trends in Hampshire churches: a chronology of St Christopher wall painting (1240 to 1530)', *Proceedings of the Hampshire Field Club and Archaeological Society*, vol. 68 (2013), pp. 85–118, p. 103

Pritchard 2016: Frances Pritchard, 'A set of late-fifteenth-century orphreys relating to Ludovico Buonvisi, a Lucchese merchant, and embroidered in a London workshop', in *Medieval Clothing and Textiles*, vol. 12 (2016), pp. 95–108

Riley 1866: Henry T. Riley, ed., *Johannis de Trokelowe et Henrici de Blaneforde: Chronica et Annales: AD 1259–1296, 1307–1324, 1392–1406* (Cambridge, 1866, reprinted 2012)

Riley 1867: Henry T. Riley, ed., *Gesta abbatum monasterii Sancti Albani, a Thoma Walsingham, regnante Ricardo Secundo, ejusdem ecclesiae praecentore, compilata, AD 793–1290*, vol. 1 (London, 1867)

Riley 1870: Henry T. Riley, ed., *Chronica Monasterii S. Albani. Annales Monasterii S. Albani a Johanne Amundesham Monacho ut videtur constripti (A.D. 1421–40)*, vol. 1 (London, 1870).

Roberts 1968: Eileen Roberts, 'The St William of York mural in St Albans abbey and *Opus Anglicanum*', *Burlington Magazine*, vol. 110 (1968), pp. 236–41

Roberts 1979: Eileen Roberts, *St William of York mural and the altar of the relics in St. Albans abbey* (London and Chichester, 1979)

Roberts 1993: Eileen Roberts, *The Wall Paintings of St Albans Abbey* (St Albans, 1993)

Roberts 1999: Eileen Roberts, *Images of Alban. Saint Alban in Art From the Earliest Times to the Present* (St Albans, 1999)

Rosewall 2008: *Roger Rosewall, Medieval Wall Paintings in English and Welsh Churches* (Woodbridge, 2008)

Rosewell 2014: Roger Rosewell, *Medieval Wall Paintings* (Oxford, 2014)

Rouse 1953: Clive Rouse, 'Paintings on the walls and timber ceiling of the central tower of St Albans cathedral', *St Albans and Hertfordshire Architectural and Archaeological Society Transactions* (1953), pp. 98–102

Rouse 1991: Clive Rouse, *Medieval Wall Paintings* (Princes Risborough, 1991)

Sandler 1986: Lucy F. Sandler, *A Survey of Manuscripts Illuminated in the British Isles, Gothic Manuscripts 1285–1385*, 5 vols (London, 1986)

Sandler 2002: Lucy F. Sandler, 'John of Metz, the *Tower of Wisdom*' in *The Medieval Craft of Memory; An Anthology of Texts and Pictures* eds Mary Carruthers and Jan M. Ziolkowski (Philadelphia, 2002), pp. 215–25

Scott 1996: Kathleen Scott, *A Survey of Manuscript illuminated in the British Isles*, vol 6, *Later Gothic Manuscripts 1390–1490* (Turnhout, 1996), no. 2, p. 34

Sharpe 2001: Richard Sharpe, 'The late antique passion of St Alban', in *Alban and St Albans: Roman and Medieval Architecture, Art and Archaeology*, eds Martin Henig and Phillip Lindley, *British Archaeological Association Conference Transactions*, vol. 24 (2001), pp. 30–37

Schildgen 2008: Brenda D. Schildgen, *Heritage or Heresy: Preservation and Destruction of Religious Art and Architecture in Europe* (New York, 2008)

Schiller 1972: Gertrud Schiller, *Iconography of Christian Art*, vol. 2, *The Passion of Christ*, trans. Janet Seligman (London, 1972)

Simpson 1980–82: Leslie Simpson, ed. and trans., 'Other doings (*Alia Acta*) of Saints Alban and Amphibalus and their companions ... by William the monk of St Albans', *Hertfordshire Archaeology*, 8 (1980–82), pp. 67–77

Sumpter 2008: Guy Sumpter, *Lady Chapels and the Manifestation of Devotion to Our Lady in Medieval England* (Leicester, 2008)

Talbot 2008: Charles H. Talbot, *The Life of Christina of Markyate*, revised by Samuel Fanous and Henrietta Leyser (Oxford, 2008)

The Builder 1864: 'The Coloured Decoration of Churches', *The Builder* (1 October 1864)

Tristram 1944: Ernest W. Tristram, *English Medieval Wall Painting: The Twelfth Century* (Oxford, 1944)

Tristram 1950: Ernest W. Tristram, *English Medieval Wall Painting: The Thirteenth Century* (Oxford, 1950)

Tristram 1955: Ernest W. Tristram and Monica Bardswell, *English Wall Painting of the Fourteenth Century*, (London, 1955)

Vaughan 1958: Richard Vaughan, *Matthew Paris* (Cambridge, 1958)

Vaughan 1984: Richard Vaughan, *Chronicles of Matthew Paris: Monastic Life in the Thirteenth Century* (Gloucester, 1984)

Wall 1913: James Wall, *Medieval Wall Paintings (The Antiquaries Primers)* (London, 1913)

Weever 1631: John Weever, *Antient funeral monuments, of Great-Britain, Ireland, and the islands adjacent. With the dissolved Monasteries therein contained...* (London, 1631)

Westhuizen 1974: John E. Van der Westhuizen, *John Lydgate: The Life of Saint Alban and Saint Amphibal* (Leiden, 1974)

Wilson 2009: Christopher Wilson, 'The architecture and ornament of the Westminster Retable as evidence of dating and origin', in *Painting and Practice, The Westminster Retable: History, Technique, Conservation*, eds Paul Binski and Ann Massing (Turnhout, 2009), pp. 79–96

NOTES

1 London, British Library, Cotton MS Nero D I, folios 2-25v; Vaughan 1958, pp.189–94; Morgan 1982, no 87, pp. 134–36
2 Roberts 1999, pp. 112–15
3 Sharpe 2001, pp. 30–37
4 Biddle 1990, pp. 124–61
5 Giles 1853, p. 460
6 London, British Library, Cotton MS Claudius E IV; Riley 1867, p. 233; Preest and Clark 2019
7 Vaughan 1984, pp. 24–25
8 Oman 1932, p. 235
9 Vaughan 1984, p. 50
10 Cherry 1992, pp. 9–10
11 Lethaby 1916, pp. 189–91
12 Binski 1992, pp. 249–78
13 Riley 1867, p. 395
14 Dublin, Trinity College, MS 177; Morgan 1982, no. 85, pp. 130–33
15 Lawrence 1996, pp. 101–06
16 Page 1902, p. 6
17 London British Library, MS Royal 2 B VI; Morgan 1982, no. 86, pp. 133–34
18 Schildgen 2008, p. 67; Rosewall 2014, pp. 13–14
19 O'Keeffe 2000, no. 26
20 Lloyd 1873a, p. 48; Riley 1866, p. xxiii
21 Michael 2017, p. 231
22 Munich, Bavarian State Library, MS CLM 835; Morgan 1982, no. 23, pp. 68–72
23 Binski 1992, p. 263, n.27
24 Coldstream 1990, p. 148
25 Lloyd 1873a, p. 21–22
26 Sandler 2002, pp. 215–25
27 Schildgen 2008, p. 67
28 Gill 2000, pp. 129–33
29 Owst 1926, pp. 45–46
30 Michael 2004, p. 13, n.8
31 Nicholson 1851, p. 31; Page 1898, pp. 35–36; Roberts 1968, p. 241
32 Gough 1786, part 2, p. 142 plate LI; The Builder 1864, pp. 684–88, fig. 2 and pp. 724–25
33 Page 1908, p. 493; Roberts 1979, p. 9
34 Howard 1993, p. 43
35 Page 1902, pp. 17–18; Roberts 1993, p. 59; Wall 1913, p. 232
36 Keyser 1883, pp. 213; Tristram 1944, 1950 and 1955
37 Perry Lithgow 1992, pp. 1–2; Howard 1993, pp. 34–45
38 Vaughan 1984, p. 47
39 Blindheim 2004, pp. 25–33
40 London, British Library, Royal MS 1D I Morgan 1988, no. 159, pp 152–54
41 Morgan 1988, no. 159, pp. 153
42 London, British Library, Additional MS 50,000, folio 7r; Morgan 1988, no 151, pp. 136–39
43 London, British Library, Additional MS 44,874; Morgan 1988, no 111, pp. 76–78
44 Michael 2017, p. 249
45 Sandler 1986, vol. 2, no. 41, pp. 47–48
46 New York, Pierpont Morgan Library, MS M 102 and London, British Library, Royal MS 3 D VI; Sandler 1986, vol. 2, no. 2, pp. 13–15 and no.4, pp. 15–16
47 Carter 1813, pl. xix, z; Buckler and Buckler 1847, p. 130
48 Lloyd 1882, p. 67
49 Munns 2016, pp. 56–58
50 Cambrai, Bibliothèque Municipale, MS 234 folio 2r and London, Victoria and Albert Museum, inv. no. 10-1873; Schiller 1972, p. 122, figs 411–14
51 London, British Library, MS Royal 2 A XXII; Morgan 1988, no. 95, pp. 49–50
52 Cambridge, Corpus Christi College, MS 53, folio 16r; Sandler 1986, vol. 2, no. 66, pp. 73–75
53 Pridgeon 2013, p. 103
54 Pridgeon 2008, p. 204
55 North 1976, vol. 2, pp. 309–60
56 Riley 1870, vol. 1, p. 448
57 Keyser 1883, p. 215
58 Lloyd 1873a, p. 17 and p. 54
59 Vaughan 1984, p. 52
60 Barron 2007, pp. 186–89
61 Pritchard 2016, p. 104
62 London, British Library, Harley MS 2255, folio 116v; MacCraken 1911, p. 137
63 Keyser 1883, p. 215
64 Vaughan 1984, p. 49
65 Dugdale 1846, p.179; Biddle 2004, pp. 6–12
66 McClure and Collins 2008, pp. 16–19
67 Luard 1874, p. 301
68 Lloyd 1873b, pp. 17–18; An alternative transcription is given in Roberts 1993, p. 19
69 Simpson 1980–82, pp. 67–77
70 Cambridge, Corpus Christi College, MS 26, page 270; Biddle 2004, p. 9, n. 14
71 Kjølbye-Biddle 2001, pp. 85–110
72 Vaughan 1984, pp. 55–56
73 Lloyd 1873b, p. 66
74 Lloyd 1873a, p. 48
75 Cambridge, Corpus Christi College, MS 7; Riley 1866, pp. xxii–xxiii
76 Oxford, Bodleian Library, Bodley MS 581, Sandler 1986, no. 151, p. 175
77 Talbot 2008, p. 40
78 Meiss 1967, vol. 1, pp. 160–69
79 London, British Library, Additional MS 29704-5; Scott, 1996, no. 2, p. 34
80 Rouse 1953, pp. 98–102
81 Harrison et al. 2012, pp. 245–72
82 O'Keeffe 2000, no. 33 (not paginated)
83 London, British Library, Cotton MS E IV; Clark 2001, pp. 218–30; Clark 2002, pp. 832–60, p. 849
84 Westhuizen 1974, p. 123
85 San Marino, Huntington Library, MS HM 19999, f.121v; Dutschke and Rouse 1989, pp. 620–23
86 Page 1899, pp. 247–48
87 London, British Library, Royal MS 2 F VII; Knowles et al. 2008, p. 96
88 Wilson 2009, p. 91
89 Windsor, Royal Library, Garter Book, RCIN 1047414 (Formerly Heraldic MS 2); Marks and Payne 1978, no. 238, p. 124
90 Biddle 1990, pp. 124–28
91 Gilbert Scott 1872, pp. 210–11
92 Micklethwaite 1872, pp. 200–03
93 Ovrey 1850, p. 86
94 London, British Library, Royal MS 2 A XXII; Morgan 1988, no. 96, pp. 49–50
95 Howard 1993, p. 43
96 Weever 1631, p. 562; Sumpter 2008, pp. 124–30
97 Fehrmann 2011, pp. 91–93
98 Kelsall 2013, p. 9
99 Duffy 2005, pp. 243–48
100 Davidson 2016, pp. 58–59
101 London, Westminster Abbey, MS 37; Sandler 1986, no. 150, pp. 172–75; Cheetham 2005, no. 179, p. 252

GLOSSARY

Alb	Long white linen tunic with narrow sleeves worn by celebrant and assistants at the mass
Amice	Rectangular white linen cloth forming a collar around the neck
Apparel	Decorated panel attached to sleeve ends, above the hem of the alb or to the amice
Antiphon	Formal response in a church service
Armorial	Heraldic, relating to coats of arms
Cartouche	Scroll-shaped ornamental tablet or panel
Chasuble	Sleeveless vestment worn by officiating priest (bell-shaped before sixteenth century)
Chevron	V-shaped stripe, often used in heraldry
Clerestory	Upper window storey in a church
Corbel	Stone bracket or support
Crenellated	Indented, shaped like a battlement
Crocketed	Decorated with leaf shapes
Cusped	Decorated with points
Dalmatic	Wide-sleeved tunic, open at the sides
Diptych	Painting or carving on two linked panels
Eucharist	Sacrament commemorating the Last Supper
Finial	Ornament at the top of an arch or gable
Gothic	Architectural style with pointed arches, used from mid-twelfth century
Lollardy	Medieval reforming church movement led by John Wycliffe
Maniple	Narrow band of cloth, often embroidered, worn over priest's left arm
Mass	Main liturgical service of the Christian Church
Nimbus	Halo, a circle of light shown behind or above the head of a saint or holy person
Ogee	Decorative S-shape or inverted S-shape
Orphrey	Decorated band (often embroidered) applied to chasuble, cope and dalmatic
Pallium	Band of white wool marked with crosses worn over the shoulders by medieval archbishops
Pier	Solid masonry support; the wall between two openings
Pilaster	Shallow rectangular pier projecting from a wall
Pinnacle	Small turret-like ornamentation at the top of a gable or tower
Quatrefoil	Carved ornament with four leaf-shaped sections or foils
Reredos	Wall or screen decoration behind an altar
Retable	Decorative altar back, often sculpted or painted on wood or masonry
Romanesque	Architectural style with round-head arches, used until the late twelfth century
Spandrel	Triangular space between an arch and linking wall
Splay	Wall indentation forming a doorway or window
Trinitarian	Relating to the Christian doctrine of the Holy Trinity: Father, Son and Holy Spirit